CONFLICTS

15 Masterpieces of Struggle and Conflict

With Exercises to Make You THINK

by Burton Goodman

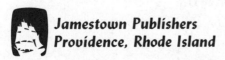

Jamestown Publishers
Providence, Rhode Island

TITLES IN THE SERIES

Conflicts

Catalog No. 875
© 1993 by Burton Goodman

Cover design by Thomas Ewing Malloy, adapted from the original
    design by Deborah Hulsey Christie
Text design by Patricia Volpe
Cover illustration by Bob Eggleton
Text illustrations by Ann G. Barrow, Jan Naimo Jones,
    Timothy C. Jones, and Lois Leonard Stock

Printed in the United States of America

1 2 3 4 5 6 7 8 9 10 BP 97 96 95 94 93

ISBN 0-89061-717-1

Contents

To the Student

This book contains 15 outstanding stories of high literary quality. As the title suggests, each selection in this volume deals with a conflict. *Conflict!* The word brings to mind images of fierce struggles, pitched battles. But while confrontation is the soul of conflict, there are many different kinds of conflicts. There is, of course, the conflict between sworn enemies or hated rivals. There may be conflict over values and ideas. Sometimes conflict is played out in a character's mind or becomes a violent clash with a force of nature. All these conflicts, and more, are represented here.

These stories will provide you with many hours of reading pleasure—and the exercises that follow offer a wide variety of ways to help you improve your reading and literature skills.

You will notice that the exercises have been specially designed to encourage you to *think:*

TELL ABOUT THE STORY

HANDLE NEW VOCABULARY WORDS

IDENTIFY STORY ELEMENTS

NOTE WORDS IN A PASSAGE

KNOW HOW TO READ CRITICALLY

There are four questions in each of these exercises. First do all the exercises. Then check your answers with your teacher. Use the scoring chart following each exercise to calculate your score for that exercise. Give yourself 5 points for each correct answer.

Since there are four questions, you can receive up to 20 points for each exercise. Use the THINK scoring chart at the end of the exercises to figure your total score. A perfect score for the exercises would equal 100 points. Keep track of how well you do by recording your score on the Progress Chart on page 158. Then record your score on the Progress Graph on page 159 to plot your progress.

TELL ABOUT THE STORY will help you improve your reading comprehension skills.

HANDLE NEW VOCABULARY WORDS will help you strengthen your vocabulary skills. Often, you will be able to figure out the meaning of an unfamiliar word by using *context clues*—the words and phrases around the word.

IDENTIFY STORY ELEMENTS will give you practice in recognizing and understanding the key elements of literature. The last question in each exercise focuses on *conflict*.

NOTE WORDS IN A PASSAGE will help you reinforce your reading *and* your vocabulary skills through the use of the cloze technique.

KNOW HOW TO READ CRITICALLY will help you sharpen your critical thinking skills. You will have opportunities to *reason* by drawing conclusions, making inferences, using story clues, and so forth.

An additional section, **Thinking for Writing and Discussion**, offers further opportunities for thoughtful discussion and creative writing.

On the following page, you will find brief definitions of some important literary terms. If you wish, refer to these definitions when you answer the questions in the section Identify Story Elements.

I feel certain you will enjoy reading the stories in this book. And the exercises that follow will help you master a number of very important skills.

Now . . . get ready for some *Conflicts!*

Burton Goodman

The Short Story—Literary Terms

Character Development: the change in a character from the beginning to the conclusion of the story.

Characterization: the ways a writer shows what a character is like. The way a character acts, speaks, thinks, and looks *characterizes* that person.

Climax: the turning point of a story.

Conflict: a struggle or difference of opinion between characters. Sometimes a character may clash with a force of nature.

Dialogue: the exact words that a character says; usually the conversation between characters.

Foreshadowing: clues that hint or suggest what will happen later in the story.

Inner Conflict: a struggle that takes place in the mind of a character.

Main Character: the person the story is mostly about.

Mood: the feeling or atmosphere that the writer creates. For example, the *mood* of a story might be joyous or suspenseful.

Motive: the reason behind a character's actions.

Narrator: the person who tells the story. Usually, the *narrator* is the writer or a character in the story.

Plot: the series of incidents or happenings in a story. The *plot* is the outline or arrangement of events.

Purpose: the reason the author wrote the story. For example, an author's *purpose* might be to amuse or entertain, to convince, or to inform.

Setting: the time and place of the action in a story; where and when the action takes place.

Style: the way in which a writer uses language. The choice and arrangement of words and sentences help to create the writer's *style.*

Theme: the main, or central idea, of a story.

1. The Most Dangerous Game

by Richard Connell

Meet the Author

Richard Connell (1893–1949) gained professional writing experience early in life when, as a boy in Poughkeepsie, New York, he covered sports for the newspaper his father edited. After graduating from Harvard, Connell served in the armed forces, and then began a highly successful writing career. Connell has written hundreds of short stories, several novels, and many film scripts, but he is probably best known as the author of "The Most Dangerous Game."

Off there to the right—somewhere—is a large island," said Whitney. "It's rather a mystery—"

"What island is it?" Rainsford asked.

"The old charts call it 'Ship-Trap Island,'" Whitney replied. "Sailors have a curious dread of the place. I don't know why. Some superstition—"

"Can't see it," remarked Rainsford, trying to peer through the dank tropical night that pressed its thick, warm blackness in upon the yacht.

"You've good eyes," said Whitney, with a laugh, "and I've seen you pick off a moose moving in the brown fall bush at four hundred yards, but even you can't see four miles or so through a moonless Caribbean night."

"Nor four yards," admitted Rainsford. "Ugh! It's like moist black velvet."

"It will be light in Rio," promised Whitney. "We should make it in a few days. I hope the jaguar guns have come. We should have some good hunting up the Amazon. Great sport, hunting."

"The best sport in the world," agreed Rainsford.

"For the hunter," amended Whitney. "Not for the jaguar."

"Don't talk rot, Whitney," said Rainsford. "You're a big-game hunter, not a philosopher. Who cares how a jaguar feels?"

"Perhaps the jaguar does," observed Whitney.

"Bah! They've no understanding."

"Even so, I rather think they understand one thing—fear. The fear of pain and the fear of death."

"Nonsense," laughed Rainsford. "This hot weather is making you soft, Whitney. Be a realist. The world is made up of two classes—the hunters and the huntees. Luckily, you and I are hunters. Do you think we've passed that island yet?"

"I can't tell in the dark. I hope so."

"Why?" asked Rainsford.

"The place has a reputation—a bad one. Didn't you notice that the crew's nerves seemed a bit jumpy today?"

"They were a bit strange, now you mention it. Even Captain Nielsen—"

"Yes. Those fishy blue eyes held a look I never saw there before. All I could get out of him was: 'This place has an evil name among seafaring men, sir.' Then he said to me, very gravely: 'Don't you feel anything?'—as if the air about us was actually poisonous. Now, you mustn't laugh when I tell you this—I did feel something like a sudden chill.

"There was no breeze. The sea was as flat as a plate-glass window. We were drawing near the island then. What I felt was a—a mental chill; a sort of sudden dread."

"Pure imagination," said Rainsford. "One superstitious sailor can taint the whole ship's company with his fear."

"Maybe. But sometimes I think sailors have an extra sense that tells them when they are in danger. Sometimes I think evil is a tangible thing—with wavelengths, just as sound and light have. An evil place can, so to speak, broadcast vibrations of evil. Anyhow, I'm glad we're getting out of this zone. Well, I think I'll turn in now, Rainsford."

"I'm not sleepy," said Rainsford. "I'm going up on the afterdeck."

"Good night, then, Rainsford. See you at breakfast."

"Right. Good night, Whitney."

There was no sound in the night as Rainsford sat there, but the muffled throb of the engine that drove the yacht swiftly through the darkness, and the swish and ripple of the wash of the propeller.

"It's so dark," he thought, "that I could sleep without closing my eyes; the night would be my eyelids—"

An abrupt sound startled him. Off to the right he heard it, and his ears, expert in such matters, could not be mistaken. Again he heard the sound, and again. Somewhere, off in the blackness, someone had fired a gun three times.

Rainsford sprang up and moved quickly to the rail, mystified. He strained his eyes in the direction from which the reports had come, but it was like trying to see through a blanket. He leaped upon the rail and balanced himself there, to get greater elevation; a short, hoarse cry came from his lips as he realized he had lost his balance. The cry was pinched off short as the blood-warm waters of the Caribbean Sea closed over his head.

He struggled up to the surface and tried to cry out, but the wash from the speeding yacht slapped him in the face and the salt water in his open mouth made him gag and strangle. Desperately he struck out with strong strokes after the receding lights of the yacht, but he stopped before he had swum fifty feet. A certain cool-headedness had come to him; it was not the first time he had been in a tight place. There was a chance that his cries could be heard by someone aboard the yacht, but that chance was slender, and grew more slender as the yacht raced on. He wrestled himself out of his clothes, and shouted with all his power. The lights of the yacht became faint and ever-vanishing fireflies; then they were blotted out entirely by the night.

Rainsford remembered the shots. They had come from the right, and he swam in that direction, swimming with slow, deliberate strokes, conserving his strength. For a seemingly endless time he fought the sea. He began to count his strokes; he could do possibly a hundred more and then—

Rainsford heard a sound. It came out of the darkness, a high screaming sound, the sound of an animal in anguish and terror.

He did not recognize the animal that made the sound; he did not try to; with fresh vitality he swam toward the sound. He heard it again; then it was cut short by another noise, crisp, staccato.

"Pistol shot," muttered Rainsford, swimming on.

Ten minutes of determined effort brought another sound to his ears—the most welcome he had ever heard—the muttering and growling of the sea breaking on a rocky shore. He was almost on the rocks before he saw them; on a night less calm he would have been shattered against them. With his remaining strength he dragged himself from the swirling waters. Jagged crags appeared; he forced himself upward, hand over hand. Gasping, his hands raw, he reached a flat place at the top. Dense jungle came down to the very edge of the cliffs. What perils that tangle of trees and underbrush might hold for him did not concern Rainsford just then. All he knew was that he was safe from his enemy, the sea, and that utter weariness was on him. He flung himself down at the jungle edge and tumbled headlong into the deepest sleep of his life.

When he opened his eyes, he knew from the position of the sun that it was late in the afternoon. Sleep had given him new vigor; a sharp hunger was picking at him. He looked about him, almost cheerfully.

"Where there are pistol shots, there are men. Where there are men, there is food," he thought. But what kind of men, he wondered, in so forbidding a place? An unbroken front of snarled and ragged jungle fringed the shore.

He saw no sign of a trail through the closely knit web of weeds and trees; it was easier to go along the shore, and Rainsford floundered along by the water. Not far from where he had landed, he stopped.

Some wounded thing, by the evidence a large animal, had thrashed about in the underbrush; the jungle weeds were crushed down and one patch of weeds was stained crimson. A small, glittering object not far away caught Rainsford's eye and he picked it up. It was an empty cartridge.

"A twenty-two," he remarked. "That's odd. It must have been a fairly large animal too. The hunter had his nerve to tackle it with a light gun. It's clear that the brute put up a fight. I suppose the first three shots I heard was when the hunter wounded it. The last shot was when he trailed it here and finished it."

He examined the ground closely and found what he had hoped to find—the print of hunting boots. They pointed along the cliff in the direction he had been going. Eagerly he hurried along, now slipping on a rotten log or a loose stone, but making headway; night was beginning to settle down on the island.

Bleak darkness was blacking out the sea and jungle when Rainsford sighted the lights. He came upon them as he turned a crook in the coastline, and his first thought was that he had come upon a village, for there were many lights. But as he forged along he saw, to his great astonishment, that all the lights were in one enormous building—a lofty structure with pointed towers plunging upward into the gloom. His eyes made out the shadowy outlines of a palatial chateau; it was set on a high bluff, and on three sides of it cliffs dived down to where the sea licked greedy lips in the shadows.

"Mirage," thought Rainsford. But it was no mirage, he found, when he opened the tall spiked iron gate. The stone steps were real enough; the massive door was real enough; yet about it all hung an air of unreality.

He lifted the knocker, and it creaked up stiffly, as if it had never before been used. He let it fall, and it startled him with its booming loudness. He thought he heard steps within; the door remained closed. Again Rainsford lifted the knocker, and let it fall. The door opened then, opened as suddenly as if it were on a spring, and Rainsford stood blinking in the river of glaring gold light that poured out. The first thing Rainsford's eyes discerned was the largest man Rainsford had ever seen—a gigantic creature, solidly made and black-bearded to the waist. In his hand the man held a long-barreled revolver, and he was pointing it straight at Rainsford's heart.

Out of the snarl of beard two small eyes regarded Rainsford.

"Don't be alarmed," said Rainsford, with a smile which he hoped was disarming. "I'm no robber. I fell off a yacht. My name is Sanger Rainsford of New York City."

The menacing look in the eyes did not change. The revolver pointed as rigidly as if the giant were a statue. He gave no sign that he understood Rainsford's words, or that he had even heard them. He was dressed in uniform, a black uniform trimmed with gray.

"I'm Sanger Rainsford of New York," Rainsford began again. "I fell off a yacht. I am hungry."

The man's only answer was to raise with his thumb the hammer of his revolver. Then Rainsford saw the man's free hand go to his forehead in a military salute, and he saw him click his heels together and stand at attention. Another man was coming down the broad marble steps, an erect, slender man in evening clothes. He advanced to Rainsford and held out his hand.

In a voice marked by a slight accent that gave it added precision, he said: "It is a very great pleasure and honor to welcome Mr. Sanger Rainsford, the celebrated hunter, to my home."

Automatically Rainsford shook the man's hand.

"I've read your book about hunting snow leopards in Tibet, you see," explained the man. "I am General Zaroff."

He was a tall man past middle age, for his hair was a vivid white; but his thick eyebrows and pointed military mustache were as black as the night from which Rainsford had come. His eyes, too, were black and very bright. He had high cheekbones, a sharp-cut nose, a spare, dark face—the face of a man used to giving orders, the face of an aristocrat. Turning to the giant in uniform, the general made a sign. The giant put away his pistol, saluted, withdrew.

"Ivan is an incredibly strong fellow," remarked the general, "but he has the misfortune to be deaf. A simple fellow, but, I'm afraid, a bit of a savage."

"Is he Russian?"

"He is a Cossack," said the general, and his smile showed red lips and pointed teeth. "So am I."

"Come," he said, "we shouldn't be chatting here. We can talk later. Now you want clothes, food, rest. You shall have them. This is a most restful spot."

Ivan had reappeared, and the general spoke to him with lips that moved but gave forth no sound.

"Follow Ivan, if you please, Mr. Rainsford," said the general. "I was about to have my dinner when you came. I'll wait for you. You'll find that my clothes will fit you, I think."

It was to a huge bedroom that Rainsford followed the silent giant. Ivan laid out an evening suit, and Rainsford, as he put it on, noticed that it came from a London tailor.

The dining room to which Ivan conducted him was, in many ways, remarkable. There was a magnificence about it, with its oak panels, its high ceiling, its vast table where twoscore men could sit down to eat. About the hall were the mounted heads of many animals—lions, tigers, elephants, moose, bears; larger or more perfect specimens Rainsford had never seen. At the great table the general was sitting, alone. Rainsford noted the table appointments were of the finest—the linen, the crystal, the silver, the china.

They were eating rich, red soup with sour cream. General Zaroff said: "We do our best here. Please forgive any lapses. We are well off the beaten track, you know."

Rainsford was finding the general a most thoughtful host. But there was one small trait of the general's that made Rainsford uncomfortable. Whenever he looked up from his plate he found the general studying him.

"Perhaps," said General Zaroff, "you were surprised that I recognized your name. You see, I read all books on hunting published in English, French, and Russian. I have but one passion in my life, Mr. Rainsford, and it is the hunt."

"You have some wonderful heads here," said Rainsford as he ate. "That Cape buffalo is the largest I ever saw."

"Oh, that fellow. Yes, he was a monster."

"Did he charge you?"

"Hurled me against a tree," said the general. "Fractured my skull. But I got the brute."

"I've always thought," said Rainsford, "that the Cape buffalo is the most dangerous of all big game."

For a moment the general did not reply; he was smiling his curious red-lipped smile. Then he said slowly: "No. You are wrong, sir. The Cape buffalo is not the most dangerous big game. Here in my preserve on this island, I hunt more dangerous game."

Rainsford expressed his surprise. "Is there big game on this island?"

The general nodded. "The biggest."

"Really?"

"Oh, it isn't here naturally, of course. I have to stock the island."

"What have you imported, General?" Rainsford asked. "Tigers?"

The general smiled. "No," he said. "Hunting tigers ceased to interest me some years ago. I exhausted their possibilities, you see. No thrill left in tigers, no real danger. I live for danger, Mr. Rainsford. We will have some capital hunting, you and I. I shall be most glad to have your society."

"But what game—" began Rainsford.

"I'll tell you," said the general. "You will be amused, I know. I think I may say, in all modesty, that I have done a rare thing. I have invented a new sensation, Mr. Rainsford.

"I was lying in my tent with a splitting headache one night when a terrible thought pushed its way into my mind. Hunting was beginning to bore me! And hunting, remember, had been my life."

"Yes," said Rainsford.

The general smiled. "I had no wish to go to pieces," he said. "I must do something. So I asked myself why the hunt no longer fascinated me. You are much younger than I am, Mr. Rainsford, and have not hunted as much, but you perhaps can guess the answer."

"What was it?"

"Simply this: hunting had ceased to be what you call 'a sporting proposition.' It had become too easy. I always got my quarry. Always. No animal had a chance with me any more. That is no boast; it is a certainty. The animal had nothing but his legs and his instinct. Instinct is no match for reason. When I thought of this, it was a tragic moment for me, I can tell you."

Rainsford leaned across the table, absorbed in what his host was saying.

"It came to me as an inspiration what I must do," the general went on.

"And that was?"

The general smiled the quiet smile of one who has faced an obstacle and surmounted it with success. "I had to invent a new animal to hunt," he said.

"A new animal? You're joking."

"Not at all," said the general. "I never joke about hunting. I needed a new animal. I found one. So I bought this island, built this house, and here I do my hunting. The island is perfect for my purposes—there are jungles with a maze of trails in them, hills, swamps—"

"But the animal, General Zaroff?"

"Oh," said the general, "it supplied me with the most exciting hunting in the world. No other hunting compares with it for an instant. Every day I hunt, and I never grow bored now, for I have a quarry with which I can match my wits."

Rainsford's bewilderment showed in his face.

"I wanted the ideal animal to hunt," explained the general. "So I said: 'What are the attributes of an ideal quarry?' And the answer was, of course: 'It must have courage, cunning, and, above all, it must be able to reason.' "

"But no animal can reason," objected Rainsford.

"My dear fellow," said the general, "there is one that can."

"But you can't mean—" gasped Rainsford.

"And why not?"

"I can't believe you are serious, General Zaroff. This is a joke."

"Why should I not be serious? I am speaking of hunting."

"Hunting? General Zaroff, what you speak of is murder."

The general laughed. "I'll wager you'll forget your notions when you go hunting with me. You've a genuine new thrill in store for you, Mr. Rainsford."

"Thank you, I'm a hunter, not a murderer."

"Dear me," said the general, "again that unpleasant word."

"Yes."

"Life is for the strong, to be lived by the strong, and, if need be, taken by the strong. The weak of the world were put here to give the strong pleasure. I am strong. If I wish to hunt, why should I not?"

"But they are men," said Rainsford hotly.

"Precisely," said the general. "That is why I use them. It gives me pleasure. They can reason. So they are dangerous."

"But where do you get them?"

The general's left eyelid fluttered down in a wink. "This island is called Ship-Trap," he answered. "Come to the window with me."

Rainsford went to the window and looked out toward the sea.

"Watch! Out there!" exclaimed the general, pointing into the night. Rainsford's eyes saw only blackness, and then, as the general pressed a button, far out to sea Rainsford saw the flash of lights.

The general chuckled. "They indicate a channel where there's none: giant rocks with razor edges crouch like a sea monster with wide-open jaws. They can crush a ship as easily as I crush this nut." He dropped a walnut on the hardwood floor and brought his heel grinding down on it. "Oh, yes," he said, casually, as if in answer to a question, "I have electricity. We try to be civilized here."

"Civilized? And you shoot down men?"

A trace of anger was in the general's black eyes, but it was there for but a second, and he said, in his most pleasant manner: "Dear me, what a righteous young man you are! I assure you I do not do the thing you suggest. I treat these visitors with every consideration. They get plenty of good food and exercise. They get into splendid physical condition. You shall see for yourself tomorrow."

"What do you mean?"

"We'll visit my training school," smiled the general. "It's in the cellar. I have about a dozen pupils down there now."

He raised his hand, and Ivan, who served as waiter, brought thick Turkish coffee.

Rainsford, with an effort, held his tongue in check.

"It's a game, you see," pursued the general. "I suggest to one of them that we go hunting. I give him a supply of food and an excellent hunting knife. I give him three hours' start. I am to follow, armed only with a pistol. If my quarry eludes me for three whole days, he wins the game. If I find him"—the general smiled—"he loses."

"Suppose he refuses to be hunted?"

"Oh," said the general, "I give him his option, of course. He need not play that game if he doesn't wish to. If he does not wish to hunt, I turn him over to Ivan. Invariably, Mr. Rainsford, invariably they choose the hunt."

"And if they win?"

The smile on the general's face widened. "To date I have not lost," he said.

Then he added, hastily: "I don't wish you to think me a braggart, Mr. Rainsford. One almost did win. I eventually had to use the dogs."

"The dogs?"

"This way, please. I'll show you."

The general steered Rainsford to a window. The lights from the windows sent a flickering illumination that made grotesque patterns on the courtyard below, and Rainsford could see moving about there a dozen or so huge black shapes; as they turned toward him, their eyes glittered greenly.

"A rather good lot, I think," observed the general. "They are let out at seven every night. If anyone should try to get into my house— or out of it—something extremely regrettable would occur to him. And now, will you come with me to the library?"

"I hope," said Rainsford, "that you will excuse me tonight, General Zaroff. I'm really not feeling at all well."

"Ah, indeed?" the general inquired. "Well, I suppose that's only natural, after your long swim. You need a good, restful night's sleep. Tomorrow you'll feel like a new man, I'll wager. Then we'll hunt, eh? I've one promising prospect—"

Rainsford was hurrying from the room.

"Sorry you can't go with me tonight," called the general. "I expect rather fair sport—a big, strong fellow. He looks resourceful— Well, good night, Mr. Rainsford; I hope you have a good night's rest."

The bed was good, and the pajamas of the softest silk, and he was tired in every fiber of his being, but nevertheless, Rainsford could not quiet his brain with sleep. He lay, eyes wide open. Once, he thought he heard steps in the corridor outside his room. He sought to throw open the door; it would not open. He went to the window and looked out. His room was high up in one of the towers. The lights of the chateau were out now, and it was dark and silent, but there was a fragment of moon, and by its light he could see, dimly, the courtyard; there, weaving in and out in the pattern of shadow, were black, noiseless forms; the hounds heard him at the window and looked up, with their green eyes. Rainsford went back to the bed and lay down. By many methods he tried to put himself to sleep. He had achieved a doze when, just as morning began to come, he heard, far off in the jungle, a pistol.

General Zaroff did not appear until luncheon. He was dressed faultlessly. He was solicitous about the state of Rainsford's health.

"As for me," sighed the general, "I do not feel so well. I am worried, Mr. Rainsford. Last night I detected traces of my old complaint."

To Rainsford's questioning glance the general said: "Boredom."

Then the general explained: "The hunting was not good last night. The fellow lost his head. He made a straight trail that offered no problems at all. That's the trouble with these sailors; they do not know how to get about in the woods. They do stupid and obvious things. It's most annoying."

"General," said Rainsford firmly, "I wish to leave this island at once."

The general raised his thick eyebrows; he seemed hurt. "But, my dear fellow," the general protested, "you've only just come. You've had no hunting—"

"I wish to go today," said Rainsford. He saw the dead black eyes of the general on him, studying him. General Zaroff's face suddenly brightened.

"Tonight," said the general, "we will hunt—you and I."

Rainsford shook his head. "No, General," he said. "I will not hunt."

The general shrugged his shoulders and delicately ate a grape. "As you wish, my friend," he said. "The choice rests entirely with you. But may I suggest that you will find my idea of sport more diverting than Ivan's?"

He nodded toward the corner to where the giant stood, scowling, his thick arms crossed on his chest.

"You don't mean—" cried Rainsford.

"My dear fellow," said the general, "have I not told you I always mean what I say about hunting? This is really an inspiration. I drink to a foe worthy of my steel—at last."

The general raised his glass, but Rainsford sat staring at him.

"You'll find this game worth playing," the general said enthusiastically. "Your brain against mine. Your woodcraft against mine. Your strength and stamina against mine. Outdoor chess! And the stake is not without value, eh?"

"And if I win—" began Rainsford huskily.

"I'll cheerfully acknowledge myself defeated if I do not find you by midnight of the third day," said General Zaroff. "My sloop will place you on the mainland near a town."

The general read what Rainsford was thinking.

"Oh, you can trust me. I will give you my word as a gentleman and a sportsman. Of course you, in turn, must agree to say nothing of your visit here."

"I'll agree to nothing of the kind," said Rainsford.

"Oh," said the general, "in that case— But why discuss that now? Three days hence we can discuss it, unless—"

Then a businesslike air animated him. "Ivan," he said, "will supply you with hunting clothes, food, a knife. I suggest you wear moccasins; they leave a poorer trail. I suggest too that you avoid the big swamp in the southeast corner of the island. We call it Death Swamp. There's quicksand there. Well, I must beg you to excuse me now. I always take a siesta after lunch. You'll hardly have time for a nap, I fear. You'll want to start, no doubt. I shall not follow till dusk. Hunting at night is so much more exciting than by day, don't you think? *Au revoir,* Mr. Rainsford, *au revoir.*"

General Zaroff, with a deep, courtly bow, strolled from the room.

From another door came Ivan. Under one arm he carried khaki hunting clothes, a sack of food, a leather sheath containing a long-bladed hunting knife; his right hand rested on a revolver in the crimson sash about his waist. . . .

Rainsford had fought his way through the bush for two hours. "I must keep my nerve. I must keep my nerve," he said through tight teeth.

He had not been entirely clearheaded when the gates snapped shut behind him. His whole idea at first was to put distance between himself and General Zaroff, and, to this end, he had plunged along, spurred on by something very like panic. Now he had got a grip on himself, had stopped, and was taking stock of himself and the situation.

He saw that straight flight was futile; inevitably it would bring him face to face with the sea. He was in a picture with a frame of water, and his operations, clearly, must take place within that frame.

"I'll give him a trail to follow," muttered Rainsford, and he struck off from the rude paths he had been following into the trackless wilderness. He executed a series of intricate loops; he doubled on his trail again and again, recalling all the lore of the fox hunt. Night found him leg-weary, with hands and face lashed by branches, on a thickly wooded ridge. He knew it would be insane to blunder on through the dark, even if he had the strength. His need for rest was imperative and he thought: "I have played the fox; now I must play the cat of the fable."

A big tree with a thick trunk and outspread branches was nearby, and, taking care to leave not the slightest mark, he climbed up, and stretching out on one of the broad limbs, after a fashion, rested. Rest brought him new confidence and almost a feeling of security. Even General Zaroff could not, he told himself, follow that complicated trail through the jungle after dark. But, perhaps. . . .

Night crawled slowly by like a wounded snake, and sleep did not visit Rainsford. Toward morning the cry of some startled bird focused Rainsford's attention in that direction. Something was coming through the bush, coming slowly, carefully, coming by the same winding way Rainsford had come. He flattened himself down on the limb, and through a screen of leaves he watched. The thing that was approaching was a man.

It was General Zaroff. He made his way along with his eyes fixed in utmost concentration on the ground before him. He paused, almost beneath the tree, dropped to his knees, and studied the ground. Rainsford's impulse was to hurl himself down like a panther, but he saw that the general's right hand held something metallic—a small automatic pistol.

The hunter shook his head several times, as if he were puzzled. Then he straightened up.

Rainsford held his breath. The general's eyes had left the ground and were traveling inch by inch up the tree. Rainsford froze there, every muscle tensed for a spring. But the sharp eyes of the hunter stopped before they reached the limb where Rainsford lay; a smile spread over his face. Then he turned his back on the tree and walked carelessly away, back along the trail he had come.

The air burst hotly from Rainsford's lungs. His first thought made him feel sick and numb. The general could follow a trail through the woods at night; he could follow an extremely difficult trail; he must have uncanny powers; only by the merest chance had he failed to see his quarry.

Rainsford's second thought was even more terrible. It sent a shudder of cold horror through his whole being. Why had the general smiled? Why had he turned back?

Rainsford did not want to believe what his reason told him was true, but the truth was as evident as the sun that had by now pushed through the morning mists. The

general was playing with him! The general was saving him for another day's sport! The Cossack was the cat; he was the mouse. Then it was that Rainsford knew the full meaning of terror.

"I will not lose my nerve. I will not."

He slid down from the tree and struck off again into the woods. His face was set and he forced his mind to function. Three hundred yards from his hiding place, he stopped where a huge, dead tree leaned on a smaller, living one. Throwing off his sack of food, Rainsford took his knife from its sheath and began to work with all his energy.

The job was finished at last, and he threw himself down behind a fallen log a hundred feet away. He did not have to wait long. The cat was coming again to play with the mouse.

Following the trail with the sureness of a bloodhound came General Zaroff. Nothing escaped those searching black eyes, no crushed blade of grass, no bent twig, no mark, no matter how faint, in the moss. So intent was the Cossack on his stalking that he was upon the thing Rainsford had made before he saw it. His foot touched the protruding bough that was the trigger. Even as he touched it, the general sensed his danger and leaped back. But he was not quite quick enough: the dead tree, delicately adjusted to rest on the cut living one, crashed down and struck the general a glancing blow on the shoulder as it fell; but for his alertness, he must have been smashed beneath it. He staggered, but he did not fall; nor did he drop his revolver. He stood there, rubbing his injured shoulder, and Rainsford, with fear again gripping his heart, heard the general's mocking laugh ring through the jungle.

"Rainsford," called the general, "if you are within sound of my voice, as I suppose you are, let me congratulate you. Not many men know how to make a Malay man-catcher. Luckily for me, I too have hunted in Malacca. You are proving interesting, Mr. Rainsford. I am going now to have my wound dressed; it's only a slight one. But I shall be back. I shall be back."

When the general, nursing his bruised shoulder, had gone, Rainsford took up his flight again. It was flight now, a desperate, hopeless flight, that carried him on for some hours. Dusk came, then darkness, and still he pressed on. The ground grew softer under his moccasins; the vegetation grew denser; insects bit him savagely. Then, as he stepped forward, his foot sank into the ooze. He tried to wrench it back, but the muck sucked viciously at his foot. With a violent effort, he tore his foot loose. He knew where he was now. Death Swamp and its quicksand.

The softness of the earth had given him an idea. He stepped back from the quicksand a dozen feet or so and began to dig.

The pit grew deeper; when it was above his shoulders, he climbed out, and from some hard saplings cut stakes and sharpened them to a fine point. These stakes he planted in the bottom of the pit with the points sticking up. With flying fingers he wove a rough carpet of weeds and branches and with it he covered the mouth of the pit. Then, wet with sweat and aching with tiredness, he crouched behind the stump of a tree.

He knew his pursuer was coming; he heard the sound of feet on the soft earth. It seemed to Rainsford that the general was coming with unusual swiftness; he was not feeling his way along, foot by foot. Rainsford, crouching there, could not see the general, nor could he see the pit. He lived a year in a minute. Then he felt an impulse to cry aloud with joy, for he heard the sharp crackle of the breaking branches as the cover of the pit gave way; he heard the sharp scream of pain as the pointed stakes found their mark. He leaped up from his place of concealment. Then he cowered back. Three feet from the pit a man was standing.

"You've done well, Rainsford," the voice of the general called. "Your Burmese tiger pit has claimed one of my best dogs. Again you score. I think, Mr. Rainsford, I'll see what you can do against my whole pack. I'm going home for a rest now. Thank you for a most amusing evening."

At daybreak Rainsford, lying near the swamp, was awakened by a sound that made him know that he had new things to learn about fear. It was a distant sound, faint and wavering, but he knew it. It was the baying of a pack of hounds.

Rainsford knew he could do one of two things. He could stay where he was and wait. That was suicide. He could flee. For a moment he stood there, thinking. An idea that held a wild chance came to him, and, tightening his belt, he headed away from the swamp.

The baying of the hounds drew nearer, then still nearer, nearer, ever nearer. On a ridge Rainsford climbed a tree. Not a quarter of a mile away, he could see the bush moving. Straining his eyes, he saw the lean figure of General Zaroff; just ahead of him Rainsford made out another figure whose wide shoulders surged through the tall jungle weeds; it was the giant Ivan, and he seemed pulled forward by some unseen force; Rainsford knew that Ivan must be holding the pack in leash.

They would be on him any minute now. His mind worked frantically. He thought of a native trick he had learned in Uganda.

He slid down the tree. He caught hold of a springy young sapling and to it he fastened his hunting knife, with the blade pointing down the trail; with a bit of wild grapevine he tied back the sapling. Then he ran for his life. The hounds raised their voices as they hit the fresh scent. Rainsford knew now how an animal at bay feels.

He had to stop to get his breath. The baying of the hounds stopped abruptly, and Rainsford's heart stopped too. They must have reached the knife.

He shinnied excitedly up a tree and looked back. His pursuers had stopped. But the hope that was in Rainsford's brain when he climbed died, for he saw in the shallow valley that General Zaroff was still on his feet. But Ivan was not. The knife, driven by the recoil of the springing tree, had not wholly failed.

Rainsford had hardly tumbled to the ground when the pack took up the cry again.

"Nerve, nerve, nerve!" he panted, as he dashed along. A blue gap showed between the trees dead ahead. Ever nearer drew the hounds. Rainsford forced himself on toward that gap. He reached it. It was the shore of the sea. Across a cove he could see the gray stone of the chateau. Twenty feet below him the sea rumbled and hissed. Rainsford hesitated. He heard the hounds. Then he leaped far out into the sea. . . .

When the general and his pack reached the place by the sea, the Cossack stopped. For some minutes he stood regarding the blue-green expanse of water. He shrugged his shoulders. General Zaroff had an exceedingly good dinner in his dining hall that evening. Two slight annoyances kept him from perfect enjoyment. One was the thought that it would be difficult to replace Ivan; the other was that his quarry had escaped him; of course the American hadn't played the game—so thought the general. In his library he read, to soothe himself. At ten he went up to his bedroom. He locked himself in. There was a little moonlight, so, before turning on his light, he went to the window and looked down at the courtyard. He could see the great hounds, and he called: "Better luck another time," to them. Then he switched on the light.

A man, who had been hiding in the curtains, was standing there.

"Rainsford!" screamed the general. "How did you get here?"

"Swam," said Rainsford. "I found it quicker than walking through the jungle."

The general sucked in his breath and smiled. "I congratulate you," he said. "You have won the game."

Rainsford did not smile. "I am still a beast at bay," he said, in a low, hoarse voice. "Get ready, General Zaroff."

The general made one of his deepest bows. "I see," he said. "Splendid! One of us is to furnish a repast[1] for the hounds. The other will sleep in this very excellent bed. On guard, Rainsford. . . ."

He had never slept in a better bed, Rainsford decided.

---

1. **repast:** meal.

TELL ABOUT THE STORY. The following questions help you check your reading comprehension. Put an *x* in the box next to each correct answer.

1. Sanger Rainsford arrived at Ship-Trap Island when
   - ☐ a. his boat landed at a dock there.
   - ☐ b. his boat crashed on the rocks there.
   - ☐ c. he fell overboard and swam there.

2. General Zaroff convinced sailors to join him in the hunt by
   - ☐ a. offering them large sums of money.
   - ☐ b. starving them until they agreed.
   - ☐ c. threatening to turn them over to Ivan.

3. Ivan was killed when he
   - ☐ a. fell into a pit.
   - ☐ b. was struck by a knife.
   - ☐ c. was shot by Rainsford.

4. At the end of the story, General Zaroff
   - ☐ a. congratulated Rainsford for winning the game.
   - ☐ b. refused to fight with Rainsford.
   - ☐ c. invited Rainsford to visit the island again.

HANDLE NEW VOCABULARY WORDS. The following questions check your vocabulary skills. Put an *x* in the box next to each correct answer.

1. Rainsford heard the high screaming sound of an animal in anguish and terror. What is the meaning of the word *anguish*?
   - ☐ a. great pain
   - ☐ b. surprise
   - ☐ c. hunger

2. General Zaroff explained to Rainsford that if the hunted man "eludes me for three whole days, he wins the game." Define the word *eludes*.
   - ☐ a. avoids or escapes
   - ☐ b. battles or fights
   - ☐ c. gives up or surrenders

3. When the door opened, Rainsford's eyes discerned the largest man he had ever seen. The word *discerned* means
   - ☐ a. wondered about.
   - ☐ b. saw clearly.
   - ☐ c. closed tightly.

4. The general smiled the smile of a man who has faced an obstacle and has surmounted it with success. Which of the following phrases best defines the word *surmounted*?
   - ☐ a. failed or been defeated by
   - ☐ b. questioned or asked about
   - ☐ c. overcome or conquered

☐ × 5 = ☐

NUMBER CORRECT   YOUR SCORE

☐ × 5 = ☐

NUMBER CORRECT   YOUR SCORE

IDENTIFY STORY ELEMENTS. The following questions check your knowledge of story elements. Put an *x* in the box next to each correct answer.

1. What is the *setting* of "The Most Dangerous Game"?
   - ☐ a. a large island in the Caribbean Sea
   - ☐ b. a swamp somewhere in Florida
   - ☐ c. a ship in the Atlantic Ocean

2. Which statement best *characterizes* General Zaroff?
   - ☐ a. He had many close friends and visited them often.
   - ☐ b. Nothing was more important to him than fine food and expensive clothing.
   - ☐ c. Hunting was to him the most important thing in life.

3. What happened last in the *plot* of the story?
   - ☐ a. Ivan gave Rainsford hunting clothes, food, and a knife.
   - ☐ b. The dead tree crashed down, striking General Zaroff on the shoulder.
   - ☐ c. Rainsford heard the approaching hounds and leaped out into the sea.

4. Which kind of *conflict* is best illustrated in "The Most Dangerous Game"?
   - ☐ a. an inner conflict that takes place in the mind of a character
   - ☐ b. a conflict between two enemies or rivals
   - ☐ c. a conflict with a force of nature

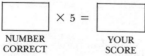

NUMBER
CORRECT   YOUR SCORE

NOTE WORDS IN A PASSAGE. The following questions use the cloze technique to check your reading comprehension. Complete the paragraph by filling in each blank with one of the words listed below. Each word appears in the story. Since there are five words and four blanks, one of the words will not be used.

Chess is among the most _____
1

and exciting games. It is played by two persons

who move pieces on a board marked with

squares. The object of the _____
2

is to force the opponent's king to surrender.

When one player's king is under attack and

cannot be defended, the other player

_____ , "Checkmate." The
3

"checkmated" player then resigns, and the

game is _____ .
4

game   courage

interesting

over   calls

NUMBER
CORRECT   YOUR SCORE

22

KNOW HOW TO READ CRITICALLY. The following questions check your critical thinking skills. Put an *x* in the box next to each correct answer.

1. The last line of the story suggests that Rainsford
   - ☐ a. killed General Zaroff in a fight to the finish.
   - ☐ b. was defeated in a fight with General Zaroff.
   - ☐ c. decided to remain on the island forever.

2. Which statement is true?
   - ☐ a. General Zaroff was not good at following a trail.
   - ☐ b. Ship-Trap Island deserved its bad reputation among sailors.
   - ☐ c. Sanger Rainsford did not have much experience hunting.

3. At their first meal together, Rainsford noticed that General Zaroff kept studying him closely. Probably the general was
   - ☐ a. deciding if he should give Rainsford his freedom.
   - ☐ b. wondering if Rainsford could escape from his room.
   - ☐ c. already thinking about the challenge of hunting Rainsford.

4. When Rainsford stepped from behind the curtain and revealed himself to General Zaroff, the general probably felt
   - ☐ a. delighted.
   - ☐ b. relieved.
   - ☐ c. shocked.

☐ × 5 = ☐

NUMBER   YOUR
CORRECT   SCORE

Thinking for Writing and Discussion

- The title of this story contains a pun—a play on words. The word *game* usually means something you play. But *game* may also refer to an animal that is hunted. Explain why the story is called "The Most Dangerous Game."
- At the beginning of the story Rainsford told Whitney, "The world is made up of two classes—the hunters and the huntees. Luckily, you and I are hunters." Show that this statement *foreshadows* what eventually happens. (*Foreshadowing* is defined on page 7.)
- Early in the story Rainsford said, "Who cares how a jaguar feels? . . . Bah! They've no understanding." Would Rainsford make that statement at the end of the story? Explain your answer.

Use the boxes below to total your scores for the exercises.

☐ **T**ELL ABOUT THE STORY

   +

☐ **H**ANDLE NEW VOCABULARY WORDS

   +

☐ **I**DENTIFY STORY ELEMENTS

   +

☐ **N**OTE WORDS IN A PASSAGE

   +

☐ **K**NOW HOW TO READ CRITICALLY

   ▼

☐ **Total Score:** Story 1

2. Raymond's Run

by Toni Cade Bambara

I don't have much work to do around the house like some girls. My mother does that. And I don't have to earn my pocket money. George runs errands for the big boys and sells Christmas cards. And anything else that's got to get done, my father does. All I have to do in life is mind my brother Raymond, which is enough.

Sometimes I slip and say my little brother Raymond. But as any fool can see he's much bigger and he's older too. But a lot of people call him my little brother 'cause he needs looking after 'cause he's not quite right. And a lot of smart mouths got lots to say about that too, especially when George was minding him. But now, if anybody has anything to say to Raymond, they have to come by me. And I don't believe in standing around with somebody in my face doing a lot of talking. I'd much rather just knock you down and take my chances even if I am a little girl with skinny arms and a squeaky voice, which is how I got the name Squeaky. And if things get too rough, I run. And as anybody can tell you, I'm the fastest thing on two feet.

Meet the Author

Toni Cade Bambara (1939–   ) was born in New York City, which serves as the setting for many of her stories. A distinguished writer, Bambara has also directed educational and social programs and has taught every level from kindergarten through college. Bambara edited the anthologies *The Black Woman* and *Tales and Stories for Black Folks.* "Raymond's Run" is from her short-story collection *Gorilla, My Love.*

There is no track meet that I don't win the first-place medal. I used to win the twenty-yard dash when I was a little kid in kindergarten. Nowadays, it's the fifty-yard dash. The big kids call me Mercury cause I'm the swiftest thing in the neighborhood. Everybody knows that—except two people who know better, my father and me. He can beat me to Amsterdam Avenue with me having a two fire-hydrant headstart and him running with his hands in his pockets and whistling. But that's private information. Cause can you imagine some thirty-five-year-old man stuffing himself into shorts to race little kids? So as far as everyone's concerned, I'm the fastest and that goes for Gretchen, too, who has put out the tale that she is going to win the first-place medal this year. Ridiculous. In the first place, no one can beat me and that's all there is to it.

I'm standing on the corner admiring the weather and about to take a stroll down Broadway so I can practice my breathing exercises, and I've got Raymond walking on the inside close to the buildings, cause he's subject to fits of fantasy and starts thinking he's a circus performer and that the curb is a tightrope strung high in the air. And sometimes after a rain he likes to step down off his tightrope right into the gutter and slosh around getting his shoes and cuffs wet. Or sometimes if you don't watch him he'll dash across traffic to the island in the middle of Broadway and give the pigeons a fit. Then I have to go behind him apologizing to all the old people sitting around trying to get some sun and getting all upset with the pigeons fluttering around them, scattering their newspapers, and upsetting the waxpaper lunches in their laps. So I keep Raymond on the inside of me, and he plays like he's driving a stage coach which is O.K. by me so long as he doesn't run me over or interrupt my breathing exercises, which I have to do on account of I'm serious about my running, and I don't care who knows it.

Now some people like to act like things come easy to them, won't let on that they practice. Not me. I'll high-prance down 34th Street like a rodeo pony to keep my knees strong. Now you take Cynthia Procter, for instance. She's just the opposite. If there's a test tomorrow, she'll say something like, "Oh, I guess I'll play handball this afternoon and watch television tonight," just to let you know she's not thinking about the test. Or like last week when she won the spelling bee for the millionth time, "A good thing you got 'receive,' Squeaky, cause I would have got it wrong. I completely forgot about the spelling bee." And she'll clutch the lace on her blouse like it was a narrow escape. Oh, brother!

As for me, I stay up all night studying the words for the spelling bee. And you can see me any time of day practicing running. I never walk if I can trot, and shame on Raymond if he can't keep up. But of course he does, cause if he hangs back someone's liable to walk up to him and get smart, or take his allowance from him.

So I'm strolling down Broadway breathing out and breathing in on counts of seven, which is my lucky number, and here comes Gretchen and her sidekicks: Mary Louise, who used to be a friend of mine when she first moved to Harlem from Baltimore, and Rosie, who is as fat as I am skinny and has a big mouth where Raymond is concerned and is too stupid to know that there is not a big deal of difference between herself and Raymond and that she can't afford to throw stones. So they are coming up Broadway and

I see right away that it's going to be one of those Dodge City scenes cause the street ain't that big and they're close to the buildings just as we are. First I think I'll step into the candy store and look over the new comics and let them pass. But that's chicken and I've got a reputation to consider. So then I think I'll just walk straight on through them or even over them if necessary. But as they get to me, they slow down. I'm ready to fight, cause like I said I don't feature a whole lot of chit-chat.

"You signing up for the Field Day races?" smiles Mary Louise, only it's not a smile at all. A dumb question like that doesn't deserve an answer. Besides, there's just me and Gretchen standing there really, so no use wasting my breath talking to shadows.

"I don't think you're going to win this time," says Rosie, trying to signify with her hands on her hips all salty.

"I always win cause I'm the best," I say straight at Gretchen who is, as far as I'm concerned, the only one talking in this ventriloquist-dummy routine. Gretchen smiles, but it's not a smile, and I'm thinking that girls never really smile at each other because they don't know how. Then they all look at Raymond who has just brought his mule team to a standstill. And they're about to see what trouble they can get into through him.

"What grade you in now, Raymond?"

"You got anything to say to my brother, you say it to me, Mary Louise Williams of Baltimore."

"What are you, his mother?" sasses Rosie.

"That's right, Fatso." So they just stand there and Gretchen shifts from one leg to the other and so do they. Then Gretchen puts her hands on her hips and is about to say something but doesn't. Then she walks around me looking

me up and down but keeps walking up Broadway, and her sidekicks follow her. So me and Raymond smile at each other and he says, "Gidyap" to his team and I continue with my breathing exercises, strolling down Broadway toward the ice man on 145th with not a care in the world.

I take my time getting to the park on Field Day because the track meet is the last thing on the program. So I always come late to the Field Day program, just in time to get my number pinned on and lie in the grass till they announce the fifty-yard dash.

I put Raymond in the little swings, which is a tight squeeze this year and will be impossible next year. Then I look around for Mr. Pearson, who pins the numbers on. I'm really looking for Gretchen if you want to know the truth, but she's not around. The park is jam-packed with parents in hats and kids in white dresses and light-blue suits. The big guys with their caps on backwards lean against the fence swirling the basketballs on the tips of their fingers, waiting for all these crazy people to clear out of the park so they can play.

Then here comes Mr. Pearson with his clipboard and his cards and pencils and whistles and safety pins and fifty million other things he's always dropping all over the place. He sticks out in a crowd as though he's on stilts. We used to call him Jack and the Beanstalk to get him mad. But I'm the only one that can outrun him and get away, and I'm too grown for that silliness now.

"Well, Squeaky," he says, checking my name off the list and handing me number seven and two pins.

"Hazel Elizabeth Deborah Parker," I correct him and tell him to write it down on his board.

"Well, Hazel Elizabeth Deborah Parker,

going to give someone else a break this year?" I squint at him real hard to see if he is seriously thinking I should lose the race on purpose just to give someone else a break. "Only six girls running this time," he continues, shaking his head sadly like it's my fault all of New York didn't turn out in sneakers. "That new girl should give you a run for your money." He looks around the park for Gretchen like a periscope in a submarine movie. "Wouldn't it be a nice gesture if you were . . . to ahhh . . ."

I give him such a look he couldn't finish putting that idea into words. I pin number seven to myself and stomp away, I'm so burnt. And I go straight for the track and stretch out on the grass. The man on the loudspeaker is calling everyone over to the track and I'm on my back looking at the sky, trying to pretend I'm in the country, but I can't because even grass in the city feels hard as sidewalk.

The twenty-yard dash takes all of two minutes cause most of the little kids don't know better than to run off the track or run the wrong way or run smack into the fence and fall down and cry. One little kid, though, has got the good sense to run straight for the white ribbon up ahead so he wins. Then the second-graders line up for the thirty-yard dash and I don't even bother to turn my head to watch cause Raphael Perez always wins. He wins before he even begins by psyching the runners, telling them they're going to trip on their shoelaces and fall on their faces or lose their shorts or something, which he doesn't really have to do since he is very fast, almost as fast as I am. After that is the forty-yard dash which I used to run when I was in first grade.

Raymond is hollering from the swings cause he knows I'm about to do my thing cause the man on the loudspeaker has just announced the fifty-yard dash, although he might just as well be giving a recipe for angel food cake cause you can hardly make out what he's sayin for the static. I get up and slip off my sweatpants and then I see Gretchen standing at the starting line, kicking her legs out. Then as I get into place I see that ole Raymond is on line on the other side of the fence, bending down with his fingers on the ground just like he knew what he was doing. I was going to yell at him but then I didn't. It burns up your energy to holler.

Every time, just before I take off in a race, I always feel like I'm in a dream, the kind of dream you have when you're sick with fever and feel all hot and weightless. I dream I'm flying over a sandy beach in the early morning sun, kissing the leaves of the trees as I fly by. And there's always the smell of apples, just like in the country when I was little and used to think I was a choo-choo train, running through the fields of corn and chugging up the hill to the orchard. And all the time I'm dreaming this, I get lighter and lighter until I'm flying over the beach again, getting blown through the sky like a feather that weighs nothing at all. But once I spread my fingers in the dirt and crouch over the Get on Your Mark, the dream goes and I am solid again and I am telling myself, Squeaky, you must win, you must win, you are the fastest thing in the world, you can even beat your father up Amsterdam if you really try. And then I feel my weight coming back just behind my knees then down to my feet then into the earth and the pistol shot explodes in my blood and I am off and weightless again, flying past the other runners, my arms pumping up and down and the whole world is quiet except for the crunch as I zoom over the gravel in the track.

I glance to my left and there is no one. To the right, a blurred Gretchen, who's got her chin jutting out as if it would win the race all by itself. And on the other side of the fence is Raymond with his arms down to his side and the palms tucked up behind him, running in his very own style, and it's the first time I ever saw that and I almost stop to watch my brother Raymond on his first run. But the white ribbon is bouncing toward me and I tear past it, racing into the distance till my feet with a mind of their own start digging up footfuls of dirt and brake me short.

Then all the kids standing on the side pile on me, banging me on the back and slapping my head with their Field Day programs, for I have won again and everybody on 151st Street can walk tall for another year.

"In first place . . ." the man on the loud-speaker is clear as a bell now. But then he pauses and the loudspeaker starts to whine. Then static. And I lean down to catch my breath and here comes Gretchen walking back, for she's overshot the finish line too, huffing and puffing with her hands on her hips taking it slow, breathing in steady time like a real pro and I sort of like her a little for the first time.

"In first place . . ." and then three or four voices get all mixed up on the loudspeaker and I dig my sneaker into the grass and stare at Gretchen who's staring back, both wondering just who did win. I can hear old Beanstalk arguing with the man on the loudspeaker about what the stopwatches say. Then I hear Raymond yanking at the fence to call me and I wave to shush him, but he keeps rattling the fence. Then like a dancer or something he starts climbing up nice and

easy but very fast. And it occurs to me, watching how smoothly he climbs hand over hand and remembering how he looked running with his arms down to his side and with the wind pulling his mouth back and his teeth showing and all, it occurred to me that Raymond would make a very fine runner. Doesn't he always keep up with me on my trots? And he surely knows how to breathe in counts of seven cause he's always doing it at the dinner table, which drives my brother George up the wall. And I'm smiling to beat the band cause if I've lost this race, or if me and Gretchen tied, or even if I've won, I can always retire as a runner and begin a whole new career as a coach with Raymond as my champion. After all, I've got a roomful of ribbons and medals and awards. But what has Raymond got to call his own?

So I stand there with my new plans, laughing out loud by this time as Raymond jumps down from the fence and runs over with his arms down to the side, which no one before him has quite mastered as a running style. And by the time he comes over I'm jumping up and down so glad to see him—my brother Raymond, a great runner in the family tradition. But of course everyone thinks I'm jumping up and down because the loudspeaker is announcing, "In first place—Miss Hazel Elizabeth Deborah Parker. In second place—Miss Gretchen P. Lewis." And I look over at Gretchen wondering what the "P" stands for. And I smile. Cause she's good, no doubt about it. Maybe she'd like to help me coach Raymond; she obviously is serious about running. And she nods to congratulate me and then she smiles. And I smile. We stand there with this big smile of respect between us. And it's real.

TELL ABOUT THE STORY. The following questions help you check your reading comprehension. Put an *x* in the box next to each correct answer.

1. Squeaky was responsible for
   - ☐ a. doing most of the work around the house.
   - ☐ b. earning money by selling Christmas cards.
   - ☐ c. looking after her brother Raymond.

2. When Mr. Pearson suggested that she might want to think about letting someone else win the race, Squeaky
   - ☐ a. grew angry.
   - ☐ b. said she would consider it.
   - ☐ c. agreed to lose on purpose.

3. Squeaky thought that Raymond
   - ☐ a. could take care of himself.
   - ☐ b. would make a very fine runner.
   - ☐ c. ran too slowly to be a champion.

4. At the conclusion of "Raymond's Run," Squeaky learned that
   - ☐ a. she and Gretchen had tied for first place.
   - ☐ b. Gretchen had won the race.
   - ☐ c. she had finished first in the race.

HANDLE NEW VOCABULARY WORDS. The following questions check your vocabulary skills. Put an *x* in the box next to each correct answer.

1. Squeaky thought that Raymond could be a great runner in the family tradition. A *tradition* may be defined as something that is
   - ☐ a. passed down from generation to generation.
   - ☐ b. new and unusual.
   - ☐ c. very beautiful and costly.

2. Because the static was so loud, nobody could hear the voice on the loudspeaker. As used here, the word *static* means
   - ☐ a. noise caused by electrical disturbances.
   - ☐ b. sweet singing.
   - ☐ c. a loud train whistle.

3. During a fit of fantasy, Raymond imagined that he was a circus performer and that the curb was a tightrope in the air. What is a *fantasy*?
   - ☐ a. a true story
   - ☐ b. a story that takes place in one's mind
   - ☐ c. a very exciting basketball game

4. Gretchen and her two sidekicks walked up Broadway together. Define the word *sidekicks*.
   - ☐ a. relatives
   - ☐ b. enemies
   - ☐ c. close friends

☐ × 5 = ☐
NUMBER CORRECT — YOUR SCORE

☐ × 5 = ☐
NUMBER CORRECT — YOUR SCORE

29

IDENTIFY STORY ELEMENTS. The following questions check your knowledge of story elements. Put an *x* in the box next to each correct answer.

1. What happened last in the *plot* of "Raymond's Run"?
   - ☐ a. Mary Louise asked Squeaky if she had signed up for the race.
   - ☐ b. Gretchen and Squeaky smiled respectfully at each other.
   - ☐ c. Squeaky noticed Raymond running in his very own style.

2. Which sentence best *characterizes* Squeaky?
   - ☐ a. She was very timid and seldom stood up for her rights.
   - ☐ b. She was certain she would win every race, so she never practiced running.
   - ☐ c. Small and skinny, she was a swift, determined runner.

3. Which statement best expresses the *theme* of the story?
   - ☐ a. A young runner realizes that coaching her brother can be as satisfying as racing.
   - ☐ b. Athletes who compete against each other must be enemies on and off the field.
   - ☐ c. If you have an unusual running style, you are not likely to be a good runner.

4. In "Raymond's Run," there is *conflict* between
   - ☐ a. Squeaky and Raymond.
   - ☐ b. Mary Louise and Gretchen.
   - ☐ c. Squeaky and Gretchen.

☐ × 5 = ☐

NUMBER CORRECT   YOUR SCORE

NOTE WORDS IN A PASSAGE. The following questions use the cloze technique to check your reading comprehension. Complete the paragraph by filling in each blank with one of the words listed below. Each word appears in the story. Since there are five words and four blanks, one of the words will not be used.

When Wilma Rudolph was only four years old, she became extremely ill and lost the use of one _____ . Doctors
                                        1
were very fearful that she might never

_____ again. However, not
        2
only did Rudolph eventually recover, but she also went on to become a world-class

_____ . She was the brightest
        3
star of the 1960 Olympic Games, winning

three gold _____ in track for
                        4
the United States.

medals   **leg**

exercises

runner   **walk**

☐ × 5 = ☐

NUMBER CORRECT   YOUR SCORE

KNOW HOW TO READ CRITICALLY. The following questions check your critical thinking skills. Put an *x* in the box next to each correct answer.

1. Clues in the story suggest that Squeaky
   - ☐ a. often complained about taking care of her brother.
   - ☐ b. decided to challenge Gretchen to another race.
   - ☐ c. loved her brother and wanted him to feel good about himself.

2. When she saw Gretchen and her friends coming up Broadway, Squeaky thought it was going to be one of those "Dodge City scenes." That phrase shows that Squeaky
   - ☐ a. thought they would all go to a movie together.
   - ☐ b. anticipated a possible fight.
   - ☐ c. became frightened and thought about running away.

3. Mary Louise probably asked Raymond what grade he was in because she was
   - ☐ a. very interested in his program at school.
   - ☐ b. curious to find out if she knew his teacher.
   - ☐ c. about to tease him.

4. Clues in "Raymond's Run" indicate that the story takes place
   - ☐ a. in Baltimore.
   - ☐ b. in New York City.
   - ☐ c. somewhere in California.

NUMBER
CORRECT

× 5 =

YOUR
SCORE

Thinking for Writing and Discussion

- Raymond was not the main character in the story, nor did he run in the race. Considering those facts, why do you think the author called the story "Raymond's Run"?
- Squeaky thought, ". . . I've got a roomful of ribbons and medals and awards. But what has Raymond got to call his own?" What does that thought reveal about the kind of person Squeaky is?
- Based on what you have read about Squeaky, do you think she would make a good coach? Do you think Raymond would make a good runner? Explain your answers.

Use the boxes below to total your scores for the exercises.

TELL ABOUT THE STORY

+

HANDLE NEW VOCABULARY WORDS

+

IDENTIFY STORY ELEMENTS

+

NOTE WORDS IN A PASSAGE

+

KNOW HOW TO READ CRITICALLY

▼

Total Score: Story 2

3. Rikki-tikki-tavi

by Rudyard Kipling

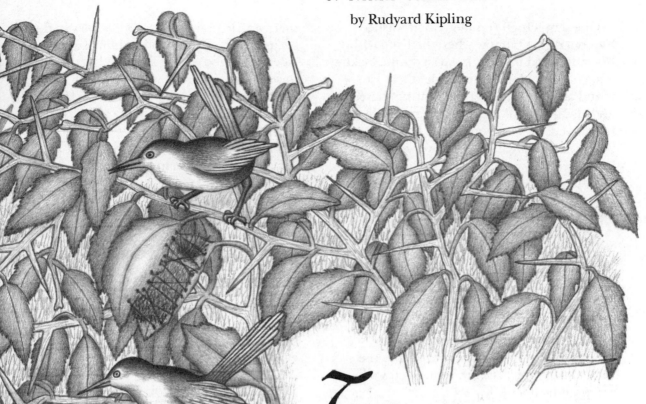

his is the story of the great war that Rikki-tikki-tavi fought single-handed, through the rooms of the big bungalow in Segowlee in India. Darzee the tailorbird helped him, and Chuchundra the muskrat, who is afraid to come out into the middle of the floor, but always creeps round by the wall, gave him advice. But Rikki-tikki did the real fighting.

Rikki-tikki was a mongoose, rather like a little cat in his fur and his tail, but quite like a weasel in his head and his habits. His eyes and the end of his restless nose were pink. He could scratch himself anywhere he pleased with any leg, front or back, that he chose to use. He could fluff up his tail till it looked like a bottle brush. And his war cry as he scuttled through the long grass was *Rikk-tikk-tikki-tikki-tchk!*

Meet the Author

Rudyard Kipling (1865–1936) was born in India, the setting of "Rikki-tikki-tavi," but spent most of his life in England. World famous for his novels, poems, and short stories, Kipling received the Nobel Prize for literature in 1907. Among his best-known works of fiction are *Kim, Captains Courageous,* and *The Jungle Books.* Kipling's most popular poems include "If" and "The Ballad of East and West."

One day, a high summer flood washed him out of the burrow where he lived with his father and mother. It carried him, kicking and clucking, down a roadside ditch. He found a little wisp of grass floating there, and clung to it till he lost his senses. When he revived, he was lying in the hot sun on the middle of a garden path, very draggled indeed, and a small boy was saying, "Here's a dead mongoose. Let's have a funeral."

"No," said his mother, "let's take him in and dry him. Perhaps he isn't really dead."

They took him into the house, and a big man picked him up between his finger and thumb and said he was not dead but half choked. So they wrapped him in a wool blanket and warmed him over a little fire, and he opened his eyes and sneezed.

"Now," said the big man (he was an Englishman who had just moved into the bungalow), "don't frighten him, and we'll see what he does."

It is the hardest thing in the world to frighten a mongoose, because he is filled from nose to tail with curiosity. The motto of all the mongoose family is *"Run and find out,"* and Rikki-tikki was a true mongoose. He looked at the wool blanket, decided that it was not good to eat, ran all around the table, sat up, put his fur in order, scratched himself, and jumped on the small boy's shoulder.

"Don't be frightened, Teddy," said his father. "That's his way of making friends."

"Ouch! He's tickling under my chin," said Teddy.

Rikki-tikki looked down between the boy's collar and neck, sniffed at his ear, and climbed down to the floor, where he sat rubbing his nose.

"Good gracious," said Teddy's mother, "and that's a wild creature! I suppose he's so tame because we've been kind to him."

"All mongooses are like that," said her husband. "If Teddy doesn't pick him up by the tail, or try to put him in a cage, he'll run in and out of the house all day long. Let's give him something to eat."

They gave him a little piece of raw meat. Rikki-tikki liked it immensely; and when it was finished, he went out into the veranda and sat in the sunshine and fluffed up his fur to make it dry to the roots. Then he felt better.

"There are more things to find out about in this house," he said to himself, "than all my family could find out in all their lives. I shall certainly stay and find out."

He spent all that day roaming over the house. He nearly drowned himself in the bathtubs, put his nose into the ink on a writing table, and burned it on the end of the big man's cigar, for he climbed up in the big man's lap to see how writing was done. At nightfall he ran into Teddy's nursery to watch how kerosene lamps were lighted, and when Teddy went to bed, Rikki-tikki climbed up too. But he was a restless companion, because he had to get up and attend to every noise all through the night, and find out what made it. Teddy's mother and father came in, the last thing, to look at their boy, and Rikki-tikki was awake on the pillow.

"I don't like that," said Teddy's mother. "He may bite the child."

"He'll do no such thing," said the father. "Teddy is safer with that little beast than if he had a bloodhound to watch him. If a snake came into the nursery now—"

But Teddy's mother wouldn't think of anything so awful.

Early in the morning Rikki-tikki came to breakfast in the veranda, riding on Teddy's shoulder, and they gave him banana and some boiled egg. He sat on all their laps one after the other, because every well brought up mongoose always hopes to be a house mongoose some day and have rooms to run about in.

Then Rikki-tikki went out into the garden to see what was to be seen. It was a large garden, only half cultivated, with huge bushes, brilliantly colored roses, lime and orange trees, clumps of bamboos, and thickets of high grass. Rikki-tikki licked his lips. "This is a splendid hunting ground," he said, and his tail grew bottle-brushy at the thought of it; and he rushed up and down the garden, sniffing here and there till he heard very sorrowful voices in a thornbush. It was Darzee the tailorbird and his wife. They had made a beautiful nest by pulling two big leaves together and filling the hollow with cotton. The nest swayed to and fro, as they sat on the rim and cried.

"What is the matter?" asked Rikki-tikki.

"We are very miserable," said Darzee. "One of our babies fell out of the nest yesterday and Nag ate him."

"H'm," said Rikki-tikki, "that is very sad—but I am a stranger here. Who is Nag?"

Darzee and his wife only cowered down in the nest without answering, for from the thick grass at the foot of the bush there came a low *hiss*—a horrid cold sound that made Rikki-tikki jump back two full feet. Then inch by inch out of the grass rose up the head and wide hood of Nag, the big black cobra, and he was five feet long from tongue to tail. When he had lifted one-third of himself clear of the ground, he stayed balancing to and fro exactly as a dandelion tuft balances in the wind, and he looked at Rikki-tikki with the wicked snake's eyes that never change their expression, whatever the snake may be thinking of.

"Who is Nag?" said he. "*I* am Nag." He spread his hood. "Look, and be afraid!"

He spread out his hood more than ever. Rikki-tikki was afraid for a minute. But it is impossible for a mongoose to stay frightened for any length of time; and though Rikki-tikki had never met a live cobra before, his mother had fed him on dead ones, and he knew that all a grown mongoose's business in life was to fight and eat snakes. Nag knew that too and, at the bottom of his cold heart, he was afraid.

"Well," said Rikki-tikki, and his tail began to fluff up again, "do you think it is right for you to eat baby birds out of a nest?"

Nag was thinking to himself, and watching the least little movement in the grass behind Rikki-tikki. He knew that mongooses in the garden meant death sooner or later for him and his family, but he wanted to get Rikki-tikki off his guard. So he dropped his head a little, and put it on one side.

"Let us talk," he said. "You eat eggs. Why should I not eat birds?"

"Behind you! Look behind you!" sang Darzee.

Rikki-tikki knew better than to waste time in staring. He jumped up in the air as high as he could go. And just under him whizzed by the head of Nagaina, Nag's wicked wife. She had crept up behind him as he was talking, to make an end of him. He heard her savage hiss as the stroke missed. He came down almost across her back, and if he had been an old mongoose, he would have known that then was the time to break her back with one bite; but he was afraid of the terrible, lashing return stroke of the cobra. He bit, indeed, but did not bite long enough; and he jumped clear of the whisking tail, leaving Nagaina wounded and angry.

"Wicked, wicked Darzee!" said Nag, stretching up as high as he could reach toward the nest in the thornbush. But Darzee had built it out of reach of snakes.

Rikki-tikki felt his eyes growing red and hot (when a mongoose's eyes grow red, he is angry); and he sat back on his tail and hind legs like a little kangaroo, and looked all round him, and chattered with rage. But Nag and Nagaina had disappeared into the grass. When a snake misses its stroke, it never says anything or gives any sign of what it means to do next. Rikki-tikki did not care to follow them, for he did not feel sure that he could manage two snakes at once. So he trotted off to the gravel path near the house, and sat down to think. It was a serious matter for him.

Some old books say that when the mongoose fights the snake and happens to get bitten, the mongoose runs off and eats some herb that cures him. That is not true. The victory is a matter of quickness of eye and quickness of foot—*snake's* blow against *mongoose's* jump—and no eye can follow the motion of a snake's head when it strikes. This makes things much more wonderful than any magic herb. Rikki-tikki knew he was a young mongoose, and it made him all the more pleased to think that he had managed to escape a blow from behind.

It gave him confidence in himself, and when Teddy came running down the path, Rikki-tikki was ready to be petted. But just as Teddy was stooping, something wriggled a little in the dust, and a tiny voice said: "Be careful. I am Death!" It was Karait, the dusty brown little snake that wiggles on the dusty earth; and *his* bite is as dangerous as the cobra's. But he is so small that nobody thinks him dangerous and so he does much more harm to people.

Rikki-tikki's eyes grew red again, and he danced up to Karait with the peculiar rocking, swaying motion that he had inherited from his family. It looks very funny, but it is so perfectly balanced a gait that you can leap off from it at any angle you please, and in dealing with snakes this is an advantage.

Rikki-tikki did not know it, but he was doing a much more dangerous thing than fighting Nag; for Karait is so small, and can turn so quickly, that unless Rikki bit him close to the back of the head, he would get the return bite in his eye or his lip. But Rikki did *not* know. His eyes were all red, and he rocked back and forth, looking for a good place to hold. Karait struck. Rikki jumped sideways and tried to rush in, but the wicked little dusty gray snake head lashed out within a fraction of Rikki-tikki's shoulder, and Rikki-tikki had to jump swiftly away.

Teddy shouted to the house, "Oh, look here! Our mongoose is killing a snake." And Rikki-tikki heard a scream from Teddy's mother. His father ran out with a stick, but by the time he came up, Karait had lunged out once too far, and Rikki-tikki had sprung, jumped on the snake's back, bitten as high up the back as he could get hold, and rolled away.

That bite paralyzed Karait, and Rikki-tikki was just going to eat him up from the tail, after the custom of his family at dinner, when he remembered that a full meal makes a slow mongoose; and if he wanted all his strength and quickness ready, he must keep himself thin. He went away for a dust bath under the bushes, while Teddy's father beat the dead Karait.

"What is the use of that?" thought Rikki-tikki. "I have settled it all."

And then Teddy's mother picked him up from the dust and hugged him, crying that he had saved Teddy from death; and Teddy's father said that he was a treasure, and Teddy looked on with big, scared eyes. Rikki-tikki was rather amused at all the fuss, which, of course, he did not understand. Teddy's mother might just as well have petted Teddy for playing in the dust. Rikki was thoroughly enjoying himself.

That night at dinner, walking to and fro among the glasses on the table, he might have stuffed himself three times over with nice things. But he remembered Nag and Nagaina, and though it was very pleasant to be patted and petted by Teddy's mother, and to sit on Teddy's shoulder, his eyes would get red from time to time, and he would go off into his long war cry of "*Rikk-tikk-tikki-tikki-tchk!*"

Teddy carried him off to bed and insisted on Rikki-tikki sleeping under his chin. Rikki-tikki was too well bred to bite or scratch, but as soon as Teddy was asleep, he went off for his nightly walk round the house; and in the dark he ran up against Chuchundra the muskrat, creeping around by the wall. Chuchundra is a brokenhearted little beast. He whimpers and cheeps all the night, trying to make up his mind to run into the middle of the room. But he never gets there.

"Don't kill me," said Chuchundra, almost weeping. "Rikki-tikki, don't kill me!"

"Do you think a snake-killer kills muskrats?" said Rikki-tikki scornfully.

"Those who kill snakes get killed by snakes," said Chuchundra, more sorrowfully than ever. "And how am I to be sure that Nag won't mistake me for you some dark night?"

"There's not the least danger," said Rikki-tikki. "But Nag is in the garden, and I know you don't go there."

"My cousin Chua the rat told me—" said Chuchundra, and then stopped.

"Told you what?"

"H'sh! Nag is everywhere, Rikki-tikki. You should have talked to Chua in the garden."

"I didn't—so you must tell me. Quick, Chuchundra, or I'll bite you!"

Chuchundra sat down and cried till the tears rolled off his whiskers. "I am very cowardly," he sobbed. "I don't have enough courage to run out into the middle of the room. H'sh! I mustn't tell you anything. Can't you *hear*, Rikki-tikki?"

Rikki-tikki listened. The house was very still, but he thought he could just catch the faintest *scratch-scratch* in the world—a noise as faint as that of a wasp walking on a windowpane—the dry scratch of a snake's scales on brick work.

"That's Nag or Nagaina," he said to himself, "and he is crawling into the bathroom through the water channel. You're right, Chuchundra; I should have talked to Chua."

He stole off to Teddy's bathroom, but there was nothing there, and then to Teddy's mother's bathroom. At the bottom of the smooth plaster wall there was a brick pulled out to make a channel for the bath water, and as Rikki-tikki stole in by the masonry curb where the bath is put, he heard Nag and Nagaina whispering together outside in the moonlight.

"When the house is emptied of people," said Nagaina to her husband, "*he* will have to go away, and then the garden will be our own again. Go in quietly, and remember that the big man who killed Karait is the first one to bite. Then come out and tell me, and we will hunt for Rikki-tikki together."

"But are you sure that there is anything to be gained by killing the people?" said Nag.

"Everything," said Nagaina. "When there were no people in the bungalow, we had no mongoose in the garden. As long as the bungalow is empty, we are king and queen of the garden; and remember that as soon as our eggs in the melon bed hatch (as they may tomorrow), our children will need room and quiet."

"I had not thought of that," said Nag. "I will go, but there is no need to hunt for Rikki-tikki afterwards. I will kill the big man and his wife, and the child if I can, and slip away quietly. Then the bungalow will be empty, and Rikki-tikki will go."

Rikki-tikki tingled all over with rage and hatred at this, and then Nag's head came through the channel, and his five feet of cold body followed it. Angry as he was, Rikki-tikki was very frightened as he saw the size of the big cobra. Nag coiled himself up, raised his head, and looked into the bathroom in the dark, and Rikki could see his eyes glitter.

"Now, if I kill him here, Nagaina will know; and if I fight him on the open floor, the odds are in his favor. What am I to do?" said Rikki-tikki-tavi.

Nag waved to and fro, and then Rikki-tikki heard him drinking from the biggest water jar that was used to fill the bath. "That is good," said the snake. "Now, when Karait was killed, the big man had a stick. He may have that stick still, but when he comes in to bathe in the morning he will not have a stick. I shall wait here till he comes. Nagaina—do you hear me?—I shall wait here beside the cool jar till daytime."

There was no answer from outside, so Rikki-tikki knew Nagaina had gone away. Nag coiled himself down, coil by coil, round the bulge at the bottom of the water jar, and Rikki-tikki stayed still as death. After an hour he began to move, muscle by muscle, toward the jar. Nag was asleep, and Rikki-tikki looked at his big back, wondering which would be the best place for a good hold. "If I don't break his back at the first jump," said Rikki, "he can still fight. And if he fights—O Rikki!" He looked at the thickness of the neck below the hood, but that was too much for him; and a bite near the tail would only make Nag savage.

"It must be the head," he said at last; "the head above the hood. And, when I am once there, I must not let go."

Then he jumped. The head was lying a little clear of the water jar, under the curve of it; and, as his teeth met, Rikki braced his back against the bulge of the red earthenware to hold down the head. This gave him just one extra second, and he made the most of it. Then he was battered to and fro as a rat is shaken by a dog—to and fro on the floor, up and down, and around in great circles, but his eyes were red and he held on as the body cartwheeled over the floor, upsetting the tin dipper and the soap dish and the brush, and banged against the tin side of the bath.

As he held, he closed his jaws tighter and tighter, for he made sure he would be banged to death; and, for the honor of his family, he preferred to be found with his teeth locked. He was dizzy, aching, and felt shaken to pieces when something went off like a thunderclap just behind him. A hot wind knocked him senseless, and red fire singed his fur. The big man had been awakened by the noise, and had fired both barrels of a shotgun into Nag just behind the hood.

Rikki-tikki held on with his eyes shut, for now he was quite sure he was dead. But the head did not move, and the big man picked him up and said, "It's the mongoose again, Alice. The little chap has saved *our* lives now."

Then Teddy's mother came in with a very white face, and saw what was left of Nag, and

Rikki-tikki dragged himself to Teddy's bedroom and spent half the rest of the night shaking himself tenderly to find out whether he really was broken into forty pieces, as he imagined.

When morning came, he was very stiff, but well pleased with his doings. "Now I have Nagaina to settle with, and she will be worse than five Nags; and there's no knowing when the eggs she spoke of will hatch. Goodness! I must go and see Darzee," he said.

Without waiting for breakfast, Rikki-tikki ran to the thornbush where Darzee was singing a song of triumph at the top of his voice. The news of Nag's death was all over the garden, for the sweeper had thrown the body on the rubbish heap.

"Oh, you stupid tuft of feathers!" said Rikki-tikki angrily. "Is this the time to sing?"

"Nag is dead—is dead—is dead!" sang Darzee. "The valiant Rikki-tikki caught him by the head and held fast. The big man fired noise at Nag, and Nag fell in two pieces! He will never kill my babies again."

"All that's true enough. But where's Nagaina?" said Rikki-tikki, looking carefully round him.

"Nagaina came to the bathroom channel and called for Nag," Darzee went on, "and Nag came out on the end of a stick—the sweeper picked him up on the end of a stick and threw him upon the rubbish heap. Let us sing about the great, the red-eyed Rikki-tikki!" And Darzee filled his throat and sang.

"If I could get up to your nest, I'd roll your babies out!" said Rikki-tikki. "You don't know when to do the right thing at the right time. You're safe enough in your nest there, but it's *war* for me, down here. Stop singing a minute, Darzee."

"For the great, the beautiful Rikki-tikki's sake I will stop," said Darzee. "What is it, O Killer of the terrible Nag?"

"For the second time, where is Nagaina?"

"On the rubbish heap by the stables, mourning for Nag. Great is Rikki-tikki with the white teeth."

"Forget my white teeth! Have you ever heard where she keeps her eggs?"

"In the melon bed, on the end nearest the wall, where the sun strikes nearly all day. She hid them there weeks ago."

"And you never thought it worthwhile to tell me? The end nearest the wall, you said?"

"Rikki-tikki, you are not going to eat her eggs?"

"Not eat exactly, no. Darzee, if you have a grain of sense you will fly off to the stables and pretend that your wing is broken, and let Nagaina chase you away to this bush. I must get to the melon bed, and if I went there now she'd see me."

Darzee was a feather-brained little fellow who could never hold more than one idea at a time in his head. And just because he knew that Nagaina's children were born in eggs like his own, he didn't think at first that it was fair to kill them. But his wife was a sensible bird, and she knew that cobra's eggs meant cobras later on. So she flew off from the nest, and left Darzee to keep the babies warm, and continue his song about the death of Nag.

She fluttered in front of Nagaina by the rubbish heap and cried out, "Oh, my wing is broken! The boy in the house threw a stone at me and broke it." Then she fluttered more desperately than ever.

Nagaina lifted up her head and hissed. "You warned Rikki-tikki when I would have killed him! Truly, you've chosen a bad place to be lame in!" And she moved toward Darzee's wife, slipping along over the dust.

"The boy broke it with a stone!" shrieked Darzee's wife.

"Well! It may be some consolation to you when you're dead to know that I shall settle accounts with the boy. My husband lies on the rubbish heap this morning, but before night the boy in the house will lie very still. What is the use of running away? I am sure to catch you. Little fool, look at me!"

Darzee's wife knew better than to do *that*, for a bird who looks at a snake's eyes gets so frightened that she cannot move. Darzee's wife fluttered on, piping sorrowfully, and never leaving the ground, and Nagaina quickened her pace.

Rikki-tikki heard them going up the path from the stables, and he raced for the end of the melon patch near the wall. There, in the warm litter above the melons, very cunningly hidden, he found twenty-five eggs with whitish skins instead of shells.

"I was not a day too soon," he said, for he could see the baby cobras curled up inside the skin, and he knew that the minute they were hatched they could each kill a man or a mongoose. He bit off the tops of the eggs as fast as he could. At last there were only three eggs left, and Rikki-tikki began to chuckle to himself, when he heard Darzee's wife screaming.

"Rikki-tikki, I led Nagaina toward the house, and she has gone into the veranda, and—oh, come quickly—she means killing!"

Rikki-tikki smashed two eggs, and tumbled backward down the melon bed with the third egg in his mouth, and rushed to the veranda as hard as he could.

Teddy and his mother and father were there at early breakfast, but Rikki-tikki saw that they were not eating anything. They sat stone-still, and their faces were white.

Nagaina was coiled up on the mat by Teddy's chair, within easy striking distance of Teddy's bare leg; and she was swaying to and fro, singing a song of triumph.

"Son of the big man that killed Nag," she hissed, "stay still. I am not ready yet. Wait a little. Keep very still, all you three! If you move I strike, and if you do not move I strike. Oh, foolish people, who killed my Nag!"

Teddy's eyes were fixed on his father, and all his father could do was to whisper, "Sit still, Teddy. You mustn't move. Teddy, keep still."

Then Rikki-tikki came up and cried, "Turn round, Nagaina. Turn and fight!"

"All in good time," said she, without moving her eyes. "I will settle my account with *you* presently. Look at your friends, Rikki-tikki. They are still and white. They are afraid. They dare not move, and if you come a step nearer I strike."

"Look at your eggs," said Rikki-tikki, "in the melon bed near the wall. Go and look, Nagaina!"

The big snake turned half around, and saw the egg on the veranda. "Ah-h! Give it to me," she said.

Rikki-tikki put his paws one on each side of the egg, and his eyes were blood-red. "What price for a snake's egg? said Rikki-tikki. "For a young cobra? For a young king cobra? For the last—the very last one left? The ants are eating all the others down by the melon bed."

Nagaina spun clear round, forgetting everything for the sake of the one egg. Rikki-tikki saw Teddy's father shoot out a big hand, catch Teddy by the shoulder, and drag him across the little table safe and out of reach of Nagaina.

"Tricked! Tricked! Tricked! *Rikk-tck-tck!*" chuckled Rikki-tikki. "The boy is safe, and it was I—I—I that caught Nag by the hood last night in the bathroom." Then he began to jump up and down, all four feet together, his head close to the floor. "He threw me to and fro, but he could not shake me off. He was dead before the big man shot him in two. I did it! *Rikki-tikki-tck-tck!* Come then, Nagaina. Come and fight with me."

Nagaina saw that she had lost her chance of killing Teddy, and the egg lay between Rikki-tikki's paws. "Give me the egg, Rikki-tikki. Give me the last of my eggs, and I will go away and never come back," she said, lowering her hood.

"Yes, you will go away, and you will never come back. For you will go to the rubbish heap with Nag. Fight! The big man has gone for his gun. Fight!"

Rikki-tikki was bounding all round Nagaina, keeping just out of reach of her stroke, his little eyes like hot coals. Nagaina gathered herself together and flung out at him. Rikki-tikki jumped up and backward. Again and again and again she struck, and each time her head came with a whack on the matting of the veranda, and she gathered herself together like a watch spring. Then Rikki-tikki danced in a circle to get behind her, and Nagaina spun round to keep her head to his head, so that the rustle of her tail on the mat sounded like dry leaves blown along by the wind.

He had forgotten the egg. It still lay on the veranda, and Nagaina came nearer and nearer to it, till at last, while Rikki-tikki was drawing breath, she caught it in her mouth, turned to the veranda steps, and flew like an arrow down the path, with Rikki-tikki behind her. Rikki-tikki knew that he must catch her, or all the trouble would begin again.

She headed straight for the long grass by the thornbush, and as he was running, Rikki-tikki heard Darzee still singing his foolish little song of triumph. But Darzee's wife was wiser. She flew off her nest as Nagaina came along, and flapped her wings about Nagaina's head. But Nagaina only lowered her hood and went on. Still, the instant's delay let Rikki-tikki catch up to her, and as she plunged into the rathole where she and Nag used to live, Rikki-tikki's little white teeth were clenched on her tail, and he held tightly on as they descended.

It was dark in the rathole, and Rikki-tikki never knew when it might widen and give Nagaina room to turn and strike at him. He held on savagely, and stuck out his feet to act as brakes on the dark slope of the hot, moist earth.

Then the grass by the mouth of the hole stopped waving, and Darzee said, "It is all over with Rikki-tikki! We must sing his death song. Valiant Rikki-tikki is dead! For Nagaina will surely kill him underground."

So he sang a very mournful song that he made up on the spur of the minute; and just as he got to the most touching part, the grass quivered again, and Rikki-tikki, covered with dirt, dragged himself out of the hole leg by leg, licking his whiskers. Darzee stopped with a little shout. Rikki-tikki shook some of the dust out of his fur and sneezed. "It is all over," he said. "Nagaina will never come out again." And the red ants that live between the grass stems heard him, and began to troop down one after another to see if he had spoken the truth.

Rikki-tikki curled himself up in the grass and slept where he was—slept and slept till it was late in the afternoon, for he had done a hard day's work.

"Now," he said, when he awoke, "I will go back to the house. Darzee will tell the garden that Nagaina is dead."

When Rikki got to the house, Teddy and

Teddy's mother and Teddy's father came out and almost cried over him; and that night he ate all that was given him till he could eat no more, and went to bed on Teddy's shoulder, where Teddy's mother saw him when she came to look late at night.

"He saved our lives and Teddy's life," she said to her husband. "Just think, he saved all our lives."

Rikki-tikki woke up with a jump, for the mongooses are light sleepers.

"Oh, it's you," said Rikki-tikki. "There's nothing to worry about. All the cobras are dead. And if they weren't, I'm here."

Rikki-tikki had a right to be proud of himself. But he did not grow too proud, and he kept that garden as a mongoose should keep it—fearlessly, with tooth and bite. And never a cobra dared show its head inside the walls.

TELL ABOUT THE STORY. The following questions help you check your reading comprehension. Put an *x* in the box next to each correct answer.

1. As soon as he saw Teddy, Rikki-tikki-tavi
   - ☐ a. bit him.
   - ☐ b. uttered his war cry to scare him.
   - ☐ c. made friends with him.

2. Nag planned to kill the big man by
   - ☐ a. waiting beside the water jar and then attacking him.
   - ☐ b. following him into the woods and then striking him.
   - ☐ c. slipping into the house at night and biting him while he slept.

3. Rikki-tikki chased after Nagaina and eventually
   - ☐ a. lost her in the tall bushes.
   - ☐ b. grew tired and went home.
   - ☐ c. caught her and killed her.

4. For as long as Rikki-tikki lived with them, the family was
   - ☐ a. very frightened of snakes.
   - ☐ b. safe from cobras.
   - ☐ c. attacked by many wild animals.

HANDLE NEW VOCABULARY WORDS. The following questions check your vocabulary skills. Put an *x* in the box next to each correct answer.

1. Darzee sang, "Nag is dead. . . . The valiant Rikki-tikki caught him. . . ." The word *valiant* means
   - ☐ a. old.
   - ☐ b. silly.
   - ☐ c. brave.

2. Rikki-tikki moved with a rocking, swaying gait that was perfectly balanced. Define the word *gait*.
   - ☐ a. a type of suitcase
   - ☐ b. the kind of steps used in walking or running
   - ☐ c. a cheerful melody

3. Hidden very cunningly in the melon patch were the cobra eggs. What is the meaning of the word *cunningly*?
   - ☐ a. cleverly
   - ☐ b. loudly
   - ☐ c. smoothly

4. When the huge cobra hissed, Darzee and his wife cowered in their nest. Which expression best defines the word *cowered*?
   - ☐ a. crouched in fear
   - ☐ b. laughed loudly
   - ☐ c. stood up

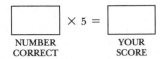

NUMBER CORRECT   × 5 =   YOUR SCORE

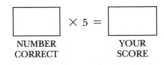

NUMBER CORRECT   × 5 =   YOUR SCORE

43

IDENTIFY STORY ELEMENTS. The following questions check your knowledge of story elements. Put an *x* in the box next to each correct answer.

1. "Rikki-tikki-tavi" is *set* in
   ☐ a. India.
   ☐ b. England.
   ☐ c. the United States.

2. What happened first in the *plot* of the story?
   ☐ a. The big man shot Nag.
   ☐ b. Nagaina grabbed the egg and began to run.
   ☐ c. A flood washed Rikki-tikki out of his burrow.

3. Who is the *main character* in the story?
   ☐ a. Rikki-tikki
   ☐ b. Nagaina
   ☐ c. Nag

4. The *conflict* in "Rikki-tikki-tavi" is best described as a
   ☐ a. fierce struggle between enemies or rivals.
   ☐ b. struggle that takes place in the mind of a character.
   ☐ c. clash with a force of nature.

NOTE WORDS IN A PASSAGE. The following questions use the cloze technique to check your reading comprehension. Complete the paragraph by filling in each blank with one of the words listed below. Each word appears in the story. Since there are five words and four blanks, one of the words will not be used.

Few snakes are as deadly and

_____ as the cobra. This
　　　　1

_____ is able to attack its
　　　2

prey in two different ways. It may use its

poisonous fangs to _____ its
　　　　　　　　　　　　3

victim, or it may squirt its poison directly

into the victim's eyes. A cobra's poison is

exceedingly powerful. It often causes

_____ within just a few hours.
　　　4

disappeared   bite

snake

dangerous   death

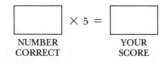

NUMBER
CORRECT

× 5 =

YOUR
SCORE

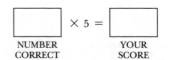

NUMBER
CORRECT

× 5 =

YOUR
SCORE

KNOW HOW TO READ CRITICALLY. The following questions check your critical thinking skills. Put an *x* in the box next to each correct answer.

1. We may infer from this story that the mongoose and the cobra
   - ☐ a. hate each other.
   - ☐ b. usually trust each other.
   - ☐ c. can live peacefully together in nature.

2. The story suggests that animals
   - ☐ a. hardly ever fight with each other.
   - ☐ b. almost never communicate with each other.
   - ☐ c. talk to each other and understand what people are saying.

3. Judging from "Rikki-tikki-tavi," you can tell that mongooses are
   - ☐ a. very cautious and fearful.
   - ☐ b. not too intelligent.
   - ☐ c. extremely active and restless.

4. Which statement is *not* true?
   - ☐ a. When a mongoose's eyes grow red, it is angry.
   - ☐ b. Teddy saved Rikki-tikki from a deadly little snake.
   - ☐ c. At times, Darzee and Chuchundra helped Rikki-tikki.

Thinking for Writing and Discussion

- Rikki-tikki, Nag, and Nagaina seem so real that it is easy to forget they are animals and not people. Do you agree or disagree with that statement? Give reasons to support your answer.
- Throughout "Rikki-tikki-tavi," the animals attempted to trick or deceive each other. Describe one scheme that succeeded and one scheme that failed.
- Suppose that Teddy was describing Rikki-tikki to a friend. What do you think Teddy would say? How would Rikki-tikki describe the family?

Use the boxes below to total your scores for the exercises.

☐ **T**ELL ABOUT THE STORY
+
☐ **H**ANDLE NEW VOCABULARY WORDS
+
☐ **I**DENTIFY STORY ELEMENTS
+
☐ **N**OTE WORDS IN A PASSAGE
+
☐ **K**NOW HOW TO READ CRITICALLY
▼
☐ **Total Score:** Story 3

☐ × 5 = ☐

NUMBER CORRECT   YOUR SCORE

4. The Mother Goose Madman

by Betty Ren Wright

Meet the Author

Betty Ren Wright (1927–   ) is one of today's most popular writers of fiction for young adults. Her novels have been honored with more than twenty major book awards, and her short stories have appeared in many leading magazines throughout the United States. Wright's family moved from Michigan to Milwaukee when she was three years old, and she has lived and worked in that city for most of her life. Wright is currently completing her thirteenth novel.

Only one thing distinguished the letter—the one that was the start of the terror—from the twenty letters she had already opened. The others were addressed to Children's Book Editor, Webster Publishing Company. This one was addressed to Julia Martell, Editor of Children's Books.

Julia noticed the distinction, but took no pleasure in it. She preferred to have her name unknown, to be anonymous in her job. That was because her job so often consisted of rejecting stories, of saying no to people. As a rule she barely glanced at the letters that accompanied the manuscripts, but turned at once to the stories themselves.

Julia opened the envelope, unfolded the single sheet of paper, and read. "Dear Miss

Muffet," the letter began. Julia sighed at this too cute approach and went on reading.

Under separate cover please find my contribution. It has been planned with you in mind and no one else. I hope it proves useful. If not, you will hear from me again. Believe me, you will.

Sincerely,

J. Smith

Curious, Julia glanced over the packages on her desk looking for one addressed in the same handwriting as the letter. It was there, stamped FRAGILE and HANDLE WITH CARE in a half-dozen places.

Fred Thompson stopped beside her desk, his arms full of art boards. He looked with amusement at the markings on the package.

"Must be worth its weight in gold," he said.

"Then it's not worth much," Julia said dryly. "It's so light that it almost feels empty."

Julia slipped off the wrappings. The box was filled with thin, feathery strips of paper, put there, it seemed, to cushion something delicate inside. Within, a bit of black color showed through. Julia moved the scraps of paper aside.

Her first reaction was disbelief. But there it was: the spider's black hairy body drawn up over folded legs, the tremor of its body as the paper was shifted. Then the legs moved.

"Oh!" she exclaimed. "Oh, *no!*"

She recoiled, because of her dread of all crawling things, while Fred slammed the heavy art boards down on the spider.

The brightly lit drugstore was just a few blocks from her home. Julia stopped there every evening on her way from the bus to pick up a newspaper. Often she would reorder the eyewash that made her hours of reading possible. Possibly she liked the store because it reminded her of the one in which she had worked during her college days. Certainly her feeling about the place had nothing to do with the clerks and pharmacist who came and left with monotonous regularity.

Now Julia waved her prescription at the white-coated man in the back of the store. She put the slip of paper on the counter, picked up a newspaper, and dropped a few coins next to the prescription.

"Anything else?" the man called to her.

"No," Julia said, but with some reluctance. The cheerful store was especially soothing after the unpleasantness of the afternoon.

Partly, of course, it was the fuss everyone had made over her that disturbed her. There was Fred, his eyes showing more concern than his comments. Then there were the copyreaders and the secretaries who had conjectured about Miss Muffet and her spider until it was time to go home. Even Mr. Webster had come in, curious about the excitement in the usually subdued editorial offices.

Julia hated their attention, which threatened to break through the barriers she had built around herself. It wasn't easy to maintain those barriers, to keep so much to herself. She knew that acting that way was not only difficult, but also probably wrong. Yet for her it was the only way. This was the way she had decided to be. It was part of the bargain she had made with herself after her husband had died.

But it was more than the attention of her co-workers that had upset her. Julia considered this as she left the store and hurried down the street to her own apartment building. And it was more than the fact of the spider. She

47

was disturbed because there was somewhere a person who called himself J. Smith, a person who, she felt, hated her with a very real hate. She, who had tried so hard to remain aloof and detached, was caught in the entanglements of another person's deep emotion.

At her apartment house, Julia opened the door of her mailbox and took out a handful of letters. There were bills. Two invitations to upcoming book conferences. A letter from her aunt, writing to thank her for a birthday present.

And an envelope addressed to Julia Martell, Editor of Children's Books.

She put the other letters into her bag, opened the door of the elevator, and stepped inside. She opened the envelope, almost eagerly. She saw at once that it was the same kind of paper with the same very thin, clear handwriting. But she also saw that the salutation was different.

Dear Miss Humpty Dumpty,

Did you enjoy my first submission? Expect another one soon.

The elevator lurched upward. Julia put out her hand to the emergency stop button, but hesitated and did not touch it. The elevator slowed, halted. The doors opened and she faced her familiar hallway with its light gray carpeting. She stepped out and waited for her heart to stop its violent thumping.

Humpty Dumpty had a great fall—

It wouldn't be, thought Julia, in the elevator, or here in the hallway, where one of the other tenants might be the victim. But it might be inside her apartment, or possibly . . .

She turned into the shadowy corner corridor that led to her own door. If she had been moving along at her usual brisk pace, she would have had a very bad fall; but caution had slowed her steps. As it was, when the wire barely brushed against her left ankle, she stopped at once. She looked closely and saw a thin, gray wire—the same shade as the carpeting—stapled to the paneling on both sides of the corridor, about three inches above the floor. From a few feet away, it could hardly be seen.

After a moment Julia took a white linen handkerchief from her bag, and draped it over the wire to serve as a warning to anyone who might be walking that way. Inside her apartment, she looked carefully in the bedroom, the kitchen, the bath. Then she came back into the living room and called the police.

The next morning, Julia took the files of rejected manuscripts into the small conference room and closed the door behind her. If, as the police believed, her correspondent was a disappointed and disgruntled amateur writer, a fanatic whose story had been rejected, she would determine his identity herself. His handwriting was distinctive—thin and clear—with unfinished loops on some of the letters, a slanted cross on the *t*'s, narrow *o*'s. She would recognize that handwriting!

In the files there was only one letter from a J. Smith. The handwriting, barely legible, was accompanied by a story about the writer's childhood. It was signed *Jack Smith, age eighty-nine.* The letter was two years old.

It doesn't seem likely he's the one, thought Julia. Patiently, she began searching through the files again. The lieutenant had warned her that J. Smith was probably a pseudonym, and common sense told her that the writer, even though he had taken no pains to disguise his handwriting, would hardly sign his own name to what could be evidence against him.

She was halfway through the third drawer of the files when the door opened and Fred came in.

"Any luck?"

She shook her head.

"Everybody's guessed what you're doing in here," he said. "And at least six people volunteered to help your secretary sort your mail this morning. They didn't find a thing."

Julia looked unhappy. "I wish they'd just forget it," she said. "The whole thing is silly. I wish *everyone* would forget it."

Her tone was sharper than she had intended, and his reply matched it. "What's eating you?" he asked, and it was as if the question had been there for a long time, waiting to be asked. "Just why—why don't you want people to care about you? Is that a crime in your book?"

They stared at each other.

"End of conversation," said Fred, after a long moment of silence. "Full stop. Now—how about dinner at Charlie's tonight—all the spaghetti you can eat and extra meatballs on request?"

"No, thanks."

"We can discuss politics; who's going to win the pennant this year."

"Thanks anyway."

Afterward, staring at the closed door, she thought how pleasant it would have been to have said yes. He was a nice fellow, fun to be with, and gentle in his way.

It was later than five o'clock before Julia had completed checking the last file. Nowhere had she come across handwriting like the writing in the letters. The day had been largely wasted. And it had taken her much longer than she had thought it would. The trouble was that she found it impossible to simply glance at the letters and put them aside. She found herself pouring over the letters, searching for any clue. J. Smith was

there somewhere. Of that she was sure.

Her secretary looked in to say she was leaving, but Julia remained at the conference table. As she had gone through the files, she had taken out every letter that made a reference to Mother Goose. These were stacked before her in a neat pile, ready to be checked again.

There were letters criticizing the rhythm of the old verses, and letters praising the Webster Company's two-volume edition. There were letters asking the meaning of a particular poem, or offering an explanation of another. One of them was written on stationery marked Ravensfoot Sanitarium, Belden, Colorado. It was dated February 11. Julia found it quite moving.

Dear Editor:

I am sending you my original *Modern Mother Goose Rhymes for Modern Children*. During my illness I have passed many hours making up these little poems which, I feel, would have appeal for today's children. I am allowed to sit up for a half-hour every day, and during that time I have copied the poems by hand. I don't mention this to gain sympathy, but to show you how deeply in earnest I am about the value of the verses. Thank you for your consideration.

The letter was signed *Dorothy Kesselman*. A note indicated that the standard printed rejection letter had been sent out on February 16.

Julia picked up the phone. "Will you get me the Ravensfoot Sanitarium in Belden, Colorado, please?" she asked the late-hours operator. "I want to speak to the doctor who

49

is caring for Dorothy Kesselman."

Julia waited, holding the letter in her hand, until the operator called her back. Then she listened without comment to what the operator said. When the operator finished speaking, Julia thanked her and asked her to call Lieutenant Schwarz at the police station.

"This is Julia Martell," she said when the lieutenant answered. "I think I have something for you to look into. A Dorothy Kesselman sent us some original Mother Goose nursery rhymes two months ago, and we returned them with our standard rejection letter. It seems she was ill with advanced tuberculosis, and she died the day she received the letter. The hospital in Colorado, where she was a patient, says her husband, Adolph, moved to this city after his wife's death."

Without question there was a touch of spring in the air when Julia got off the bus that night and walked up the block. In front of the old brick houses near the corner a forsythia was beginning to bloom, its yellow buds poking above the green. Julia looked at the narrow windows of the houses and wondered about the people behind them. Were they happy? Were they lonely? Had any of them ever noticed her as she returned night after night?

At the drugstore, one of the women who worked part time was behind the counter. Julia collected a paper, some magazines, and her medicine, which was wrapped and waiting for her.

"How are you tonight?" Julia asked as she paid for the items, and was aware that the woman stared in surprise at the greeting. "It's spring," Julia added, foolishly.

Outside again, Julia walked quickly toward her apartment building. When she entered the foyer, she tried to pass the mailbox without looking into it. But she could not ignore the white envelope seen through the little slot in the box.

Dear Miss Peep-Peep,

I don't know if you are much of a swimmer or a mountain climber, but it doesn't matter. The name fits—or soon will. This is my last submission, one which you have earned by your sympathy, your compassion, and your understanding.

Sincerely,

J. Smith

Julia read the letter twice. Then she rang for the elevator and rode up to her floor. She crossed the corridor with slow, careful steps, ones designed to reveal any invisible obstacles. When she opened the door, she stood back a moment before going inside.

It could be anything this time. She had never heard of Peep-Peep.

The living room appeared just as she had left it. She looked around the rest of the apartment, and then with her coat still on, took her *Complete Mother Goose* from the shelf and thumbed through the index. It was there— a short riddle-rhyme about a star:

I have a little sister, they call her Peep-Peep;
She wades the waters deep, deep, deep;
She climbs the mountains high, high, high;
Poor little creature, she has but one eye.

The telephone rang. Julia picked it up and heard the voice of Lieutenant Schwarz.

"You can relax," he told Julia. "We've got

your joker. Picked him up right after you called us. Good thing you tipped us off. You were right on the money. The husband of the Mrs. Kesselman who wrote you—he admitted it right away. Went off the deep end after his wife died. He says she worked for six months on the poems she sent you, and you didn't even— Well, he seems to think that if you'd sent a word of encouragement instead of a form letter, it would have made a difference. She was practically staying alive for your answer, according to him, and when it came—she just gave up."

Julia leaned back. "Yes," she said, "I'm sorry about that. I understand you, Lieutenant. But it wasn't fair, was it? I mean, to put all that responsibility on me—"

The lieutenant sounded uncomfortable. "He says he wrote a letter that should have tipped you off," he said. "He knew he was going to be caught at this, but he didn't care. Anyway, you don't have to worry any more."

"Do I know him?"

"Could be." Lieutenant Schwarz seemed relieved to get off the delicate subject of motive. "At least, you've *seen* him. He's the pharmacist in the drugstore just down the block from your place."

Julia returned the receiver to its hook and sat for a long time in thought, without moving. Then she picked up the bottle of eyewash from the coffee table and unwrapped it. Her handkerchief was lying on the table, and she poured a little of the liquid from the bottle onto the cloth. The spot widened and then, as she watched, the dampened area shredded and dissolved. Through the small round hole, she saw the wood of the coffee table turn yellow.

Poor little creature, she had but one eye. Julia looked around the room that had been for a long time her cheerful, safe retreat. Then she picked up the telephone directory and began turning the pages.

"Fred," she said a moment later. "This is Julia. Are the spaghetti and meatballs still available? I think I'd like them very much."

TELL ABOUT THE STORY. The following questions help you check your reading comprehension. Put an *x* in the box next to each correct answer.

1. On her way home from the bus, Julia Martell stopped at the drugstore to
   - ☐ a. pick up a newspaper and sometimes order eyewash.
   - ☐ b. purchase a sandwich to eat at home later.
   - ☐ c. call Lieutenant Schwarz to find out about the case.

2. After Julia received a letter addressed to "Miss Humpty Dumpty," she looked for something that might make her
   - ☐ a. laugh.
   - ☐ b. fall.
   - ☐ c. relax.

3. Mr. Kesselman was very angry with Julia because she
   - ☐ a. refused to read a story he had sent her.
   - ☐ b. rejected his wife's poems with a discouraging form letter.
   - ☐ c. bought just a few items in the drugstore where he worked.

4. At the conclusion of "The Mother Goose Madman," Julia decided to
   - ☐ a. leave her job.
   - ☐ b. write a letter to Mr. Kesselman.
   - ☐ c. go out with Fred Thompson.

HANDLE NEW VOCABULARY WORDS. The following questions check your vocabulary skills. Put an *x* in the box next to each correct answer.

1. Everyone was curious about all the excitement in the office, which was usually so subdued. As used here, the word *subdued* means
   - ☐ a. quiet.
   - ☐ b. noisy.
   - ☐ c. clean.

2. When Julia saw the spider, she recoiled because of her dread of all crawling things. The word *recoiled* means
   - ☐ a. laughed loudly.
   - ☐ b. coughed.
   - ☐ c. drew back.

3. The police thought that the threatening letter was sent by a disappointed and disgruntled writer. Define the word *disgruntled.*
   - ☐ a. charming
   - ☐ b. unhappy
   - ☐ c. delighted

4. She saw the tremor of the spider's body as its legs moved. What is the meaning of the word *tremor*?
   - ☐ a. shaking
   - ☐ b. weakness
   - ☐ c. sadness

☐ × 5 = ☐

NUMBER CORRECT   YOUR SCORE

☐ × 5 = ☐

NUMBER CORRECT   YOUR SCORE

IDENTIFY STORY ELEMENTS. The following questions check your knowledge of story elements. Put an *x* in the box next to each correct answer.

1. Who is the *main character* in "The Mother Goose Madman"?
   □ a. Dorothy Kesselman
   □ b. Fred Thompson
   □ c. Julia Martell

2. What happened first in the *plot* of the story?
   □ a. Julia read a letter sent from the Ravensfoot Sanitarium.
   □ b. Lieutenant Schwarz told Julia, "We've got your joker."
   □ c. Julia received a package containing a spider.

3. Select the statement that best expresses the *theme* of "The Mother Goose Madman."
   □ a. A close call with disaster changes a young woman's attitude toward life.
   □ b. Editors should accept all the stories they receive to prevent making enemies.
   □ c. Almost every crime can be solved if there is sufficient evidence available.

4. In this story, the main *conflict* is between
   □ a. an editor and someone who wants to harm her.
   □ b. an editor and a police lieutenant.
   □ c. a clerk and a pharmacist in a drugstore.

	× 5 =	
NUMBER CORRECT		YOUR SCORE

NOTE WORDS IN A PASSAGE. The following questions use the cloze technique to check your reading comprehension. Complete the paragraph by filling in each blank with one of the words listed below. Each word appears in the story. Since there are five words and four blanks, one of the words will not be used.

Down through the years, countless numbers of _____ have enjoyed the
1
Mother Goose nursery rhymes. Scholars have attempted to _____ whether
2
Mother Goose ever really lived. The _____ available suggests that
3
Mother Goose was not a real person but was the creation of someone's imagination. In any case, the _____ and tales
4
that bear her name provide much pleasure to children around the world.

determine   children

evidence

verses   correspondent

	× 5 =	
NUMBER CORRECT		YOUR SCORE

KNOW HOW TO READ CRITICALLY. The following questions check your critical thinking skills. Put an *x* in the box next to each correct answer.

1. We may infer that the "eyewash" Julia brought home at the end of the story was actually
   ☐ a. a harmless liquid.
   ☐ b. nothing more than water.
   ☐ c. a powerful acid.

2. Apparently, Mr. Kesselman wanted to injure Julia because he believed that she
   ☐ a. had reported him to the police.
   ☐ b. had been stealing items from the drugstore.
   ☐ c. was responsible for hastening the death of his wife.

3. What is true of the last two letters that Julia received?
   ☐ a. Each contained a clue to the danger ahead.
   ☐ b. Each was signed "A. Kesselman."
   ☐ c. Each was addressed to "J. Martell."

4. The last paragraph of the story suggests that Julia decided to
   ☐ a. break out of the shell she had constructed around herself.
   ☐ b. tell Fred that she didn't want to go out with him.
   ☐ c. eat out every night from then on.

Thinking for Writing and Discussion

- Who was "The Mother Goose Madman"? Present several examples as evidence to support your answer.
- Dorothy Kesselman was upset that Julia sent a standard form letter rejecting her poems. Suppose that Julia rejected the poems with a letter that was personal and encouraging. What might the letter have said? (Refer to Dorothy's letter to Julia when considering your answer.)
- Describe Julia's *character development*— the way she changed from the beginning to the conclusion of the story. Offer specific examples.

Use the boxes below to total your scores for the exercises.

☐ **T**ELL ABOUT THE STORY
+
☐ **H**ANDLE NEW VOCABULARY WORDS
+
☐ **I**DENTIFY STORY ELEMENTS
+
☐ **N**OTE WORDS IN A PASSAGE
+
☐ **K**NOW HOW TO READ CRITICALLY
▼
☐ **Total Score:** Story 4

☐ × 5 = ☐
NUMBER   YOUR
CORRECT   SCORE

5. Split Cherry Tree

by Jesse Stuart

Meet the Author

Jesse Stuart (1907–1984) was born in the Kentucky hill country. He lived and worked on a small farm there, and as a young man, taught in a small school similar to the one in "Split Cherry Tree." Drawing from his experiences growing up in Kentucky, Stuart wrote a popular autobiographical novel, *The Thread That Runs So True.* He has also authored hundreds of short stories, numerous poems, and many articles and books.

I don't mind staying after school," I says to Professor Herbert, "but I'd rather you'd whip me with a switch and let me go home early. Pa will whip me anyway for getting home two hours late."

"You are too big to whip," says Professor Herbert, "and I have to punish you for climbing up in that cherry tree. You boys knew better than that! The other five boys have paid their dollar each. You have been the only one who has not helped pay for the tree. Can't you borrow a dollar?"

"I can't," I says. "I'll have to take the punishment. I wish it would be quicker punishment. I wouldn't mind."

Professor Herbert stood and looked at me. He was a big man. He wore a gray suit of clothes. The suit matched his gray hair.

"You don't know my father," I says to Professor Herbert. "He might be called a little old-fashioned. He makes us mind him until we're twenty-one years old. He believes if you spare the rod you spoil the child. I'll never be able to make him understand about the cherry tree. I'm the first of my people to go to high school."

"You must take the punishment," says

Professor Herbert. "You must stay two hours after school today and two hours after school tomorrow. I am allowing you twenty-five cents an hour. That is good money for a high school student. You can sweep the schoolhouse floor, wash the blackboards, and clean windows. I'll pay the dollar for you."

I couldn't ask Professor Herbert to loan me a dollar. He never offered to loan it to me. I had to stay and help the janitor and work out my fine at a quarter an hour.

I thought as I swept the floor, "What will Pa do to me? What lie can I tell him when I go home? Why did we ever climb that cherry tree and break it down for anyway? Why did we run crazy over the hills away from the crowd? Why did we do all of this? Six of us climbed up in a little cherry tree after one little lizard! Why did the tree split and fall with us? It should have been a stronger tree! Why did Eif Crabtree just happen to be below us plowing and catch us in his cherry tree? Why wasn't he a better man than to charge us six dollars for the tree?"

It was six o'clock when I left the schoolhouse. I had six miles to walk home. It would be after seven when I got home. I had all my work to do when I got home. It took Pa and me both to do the work. Seven cows to milk. Nineteen head of cattle to feed, four mules, twenty-five hogs, firewood and stovewood to cut, and water to draw from the well. He would be doing it when I got home. He would be mad and wondering what was keeping me!

I hurried home. I would run under the dark, leafless trees. I would walk fast uphill. I would run down the hill. The ground was freezing. I had to hurry. I had to run. I reached the long ridge that led to our cow pasture. I ran along this ridge. The wind dried the sweat on my face. I ran across the pasture to the house.

I threw down my books in the chipyard. I ran to the barn to spread fodder on the ground for the cattle. I didn't take time to change my clean school clothes for my old work clothes. I ran out to the barn. I saw Pa spreading fodder on the ground to the cattle. That was my job. I ran up to the fence. I says, "Leave that for me, Pa. I'll do it, I'm just a little late."

"I see you are," says Pa. He turned and looked at me. His eyes danced fire. "What in th' world has kept you so? Why ain't you been here to help me with this work? Make a gentleman out'n one boy in th' family and this is what you get! Send you to high school and you get too onery fer th' buzzards to smell!"

I never said anything. I didn't want to tell why I was late from school. Pa stopped scattering the bundles of fodder. He looked at me. He says, "Why are you gettin' in here this time o' night? You tell me or I'll take a hickory withe to you right here on th' spot!"

I says, "I had to stay after school." I couldn't lie to Pa. He'd go to school and find out why I had to stay. If I lied to him it would be too bad for me.

"Why did you haf to stay atter school?" says Pa.

I says, "Our biology class went on a field trip today. Six of us boys broke down a cherry tree. We had to give a dollar apiece to pay for the tree. I didn't have the dollar. Professor Herbert is making me work out my dollar. He gives me twenty-five cents an hour. I had to stay in this afternoon. I'll have to stay in tomorrow afternoon!"

"Are you telling me th' truth?" says Pa.

"I'm telling you the truth," I says. "Go and see for yourself."

"That's jist what I'll do in th' mornin'," says

Pa. "Jist whose cherry tree did you break down?"

"Eif Crabtree's cherry tree!"

"What was you doin' clear out in Eif Crabtree's place?" says Pa. "He lives four miles from th' county high school. Don't they teach you no books at that high school? Do they jist let you get out and gad over th' hillsides? If that's all they do I'll keep you at home, Dave. I've got work here fer you to do!"

"Pa," I says, "spring is just getting here. We take a subject in school where we have to have bugs, snakes, flowers, lizards, frogs, and plants. It is biology. It was a pretty day today. We went out to find a few of these. Six of us boys saw a lizard at the same time sunning on a cherry tree. We all went up the tree to get it. We broke the tree down. It split at the forks. Eif Crabtree was plowing down below us. He ran up the hill and got our names. The other boys gave their dollar apiece. I didn't have mine. Professor Herbert put mine in for me. I have to work it out at school."

"Poor man's son, huh," says Pa. "I'll attend to that myself in th' mornin'. I'll take keer o' 'im. He ain't from this county nohow. I'll go down there in th' mornin' and see 'im. Lettin' you leave your books and gallivant all over th' hills. What kind of a school is it nohow! Didn't do that, my son, when I's a little shaver in school. All fared alike, too."

"Pa, please don't go down there," I says, "just let me have fifty cents and pay the rest of my fine! I don't want you to go down there! I don't want you to start anything with Professor Herbert!"

"Ashamed of your old Pap, are you, Dave," says Pa, "atter th' way I've worked to raise you! Tryin' to send you to school so you can make a better livin' than I've made.

"I'll straighten this thing out myself! I'll take keer o' Professor Herbert myself! He ain't got no right to keep you in and let the other boys off jist because they've got th' money! I'm a poor man. A bullet will go in a professor same as it will any man. It will go in a rich man same as it will a poor man. Now you get into this work before I take one o' these withes and cut the shirt off'n your back!"

I could tell Pa that school had changed in the hills from the way it was when he was a boy, but he wouldn't understand. I could tell him we studied frogs, birds, snakes, lizards, flowers, insects. But Pa wouldn't understand. He would see Professor Herbert anyway. I'd just have to finish foddering the cattle and go to school with Pa the next morning.

I finished my work by moonlight. Professor Herbert really didn't know how much work I had to do at home. If he had known he would not have kept me after school. He would have loaned me a dollar to have paid my part on the cherry tree. He had never lived in the hills. He didn't know the way the hill boys had to work so that they could go to school. Now he was teaching in a county high school where all the boys who attended were from hill farms.

After I'd finished doing my work I went to the house and ate my supper. Pa and Mom had eaten. My supper was getting cold. I heard Pa and Mom talking in the front room. Pa was telling Mom about me staying in after school.

"I had to do all th' milkin' tonight, chop th' wood myself. It's too hard on me atter I've turned ground all day. I'm goin' to take a day off tomorrow and see if I can't remedy things a little. I'll go down to that high school tomorrow. I won't be a very good scholar fer Professor Herbert nohow. He won't keep me in atter school. I'll take a different kind of lesson down there and make 'im acquainted with it."

"Now, Luster," says Mom, "you jist stay away

from there. Don't cause a lot o' trouble. You can be jailed fer a trick like that. You'll get th' Law atter you. You'll just go down there and show off and plague your own boy Dave to death in front o' all th' scholars!"

"Plague or no plague," says Pa, "he don't take into consideration what all I haf to do here, does he? I'll show 'im it ain't right to keep one boy in and let the rest go scot-free. My boy is good as th' rest, ain't he? A bullet will make a hole in a schoolteacher same as it will anybody else. He can't do me that way and get by with it. I'll plug 'im first. I aim to go down there bright and early in the mornin' and get all this straight!"

I ate my supper. I slipped upstairs and lit the lamp. I tried to forget the whole thing. I studied plane geometry. Then I studied my biology lesson. I could hardly study for thinking about Pa. "He'll go to school with me in the morning. He'll take a gun for Professor Herbert! What will Professor Herbert think of me! I'll tell him when Pa leaves that I couldn't help it. But Pa might shoot him. I hate to go with Pa. Maybe he'll cool off about it tonight and not go in the morning."

Pa got up at four o'clock. He built a fire in the stove. Then he built a fire in the fire-place. He got Mom up to get breakfast. Then he got me up to help feed and milk. By the time we had our work done at the barn, Mom had breakfast ready for us. We ate our breakfast. Daylight came and we could see the bare oak trees covered white with frost. The hills were white with frost. A cold wind was blowing.

"Now, Dave," says Pa, "let's get ready fer school. I aim to go with you this mornin' and look into bug larnin', frog larnin', lizard and snake larnin', and breakin' down cherry trees!

I don't like no sicha foolish way o' larnin' myself!"

Pa hadn't forgot. I'd have to take him to school with me. He would take me to school with him. We were going early. I was glad we were going early. If Pa pulled a gun on Professor Herbert there wouldn't be so many of my classmates there to see him.

I knew that Pa wouldn't be at home in the high school. He wore overalls, big boots, a blue shirt and a sheepskin coat, and a slouched black hat gone to seed at the top. He put his gun in its holster. We started trudging toward the high school across the hill.

It was early when we got to the county high school. Professor Herbert had just got there. I just thought as we walked up the steps into the schoolhouse, "Maybe Pa will find out Professor Herbert is a good man. He just doesn't know him. Just like I felt toward the Lambert boys across the hill. I didn't like them until I'd seen them and talked to them. After I went to school with them and talked to them, I liked them and we were friends. It's a lot in knowing the other fellow."

"You're th' Professor here, ain't you?" says Pa.

"Yes," says Professor Herbert, "and you are Dave's father."

"Yes," says Pa, pulling out his gun and laying it on the seat in Professor Herbert's office. Professor Herbert's eyes got big behind his black-rimmed glasses when he saw Pa's gun. Color came into his pale cheeks.

"Jist a few things about this school I want to know," says Pa. "I'm tryin' to make a scholar out'n Dave. He's the only one out'n eleven youngins I've sent to high school. Here he comes in late and leaves me all th' work to do! He said you's all out bug huntin' yesterday and broke a cherry tree down. He had to stay two hours atter school yesterday and work out money to pay on that cherry tree! Is that right?"

"Wwwwy," says Professor Herbert, "I guess it is."

He looked at Pa's gun.

"Well," says Pa, "this ain't no high school. It's a bug school, a lizard school, a snake school! It ain't no school nohow!"

"Why did you bring that gun?" says Professor Herbert to Pa.

"You see that little hole," says Pa as he picked up the long blue forty-four and put his finger on the end of the barrel, "a bullet can come out'n that hole that will kill a school-teacher same as it will any other man. It will kill a rich man same as a poor man. It will kill a man. But atter I come in and saw you, I know'd I wouldn't need it. This maul[1] o' mine could do you up in a few minutes."

Pa stood there, big, hard, brown-skinned, and mighty, beside of Professor Herbert. I didn't know Pa was so much bigger. I'd never seen Pa in a schoolhouse before. I'd seen Professor Herbert. He always looked big before to me. He didn't look big standing beside of Pa.

"I was only doing my duty, Mr. Sexton," says Professor Herbert, "and following the course of study the state provided us with."

"Course o' study," says Pa, "what study, bug study? Varmint study?"

Students were coming into the school-house now.

Professor Herbert says, "Close the door, Dave, so others won't hear."

I walked over and closed the door. I was shaking like a leaf in the wind. I thought Pa was going to hit Professor Herbert every minute. He was doing all the talking. His

face was getting red. The red color was coming through the brown, weather-beaten skin on Pa's face.

"It jist don't look good to me," says Pa, "a-takin' all this swarm of youngins out to pillage th' whole deestrict. Breakin' down cherry trees. Keepin' boys in atter school."

"What else could I have done with Dave, Mr. Sexton?" says Professor Herbert. "The boys didn't have any business all climbing that cherry tree after one lizard. One boy could have gone up in the tree and got it. The farmer charged us six dollars. It was a little steep, I think, but we had it to pay. Must I make five boys pay and let your boy off? He said he didn't have the dollar and couldn't get it. So I put it in for him. I'm letting him work it out. He's not working for me. He's working for the school!"

"I jist don't know what you could a-done with 'im," says Pa, "only a-larruped 'im with a withe! That's what he needed!"

"He's too big to whip," says Professor Herbert, pointing at me. "He's a man in size."

"He's not too big fer me to whip," says Pa. "They ain't too big until they're over twenty-one! It jist didn't look fair to me! Work one and let th' rest out because they got th' money. I don't see what bugs has got to do with a high school! It don't look good to me nohow!"

Pa picked up his gun and put it back in its holster. The red color left Professor Herbert's face. He talked more to Pa. Pa softened a little. It looked funny to see Pa in the high school building. It was the first time he'd ever been there.

"We were not only hunting snakes, toads, flowers, butterflies, lizards," says Professor Herbert, "but, Mr. Sexton, I was hunting dry timothy grass to put in an incubator and raise some protozoa."

---

1. **maul:** a very heavy hammer. Here Pa means his fist.

59

"I don't know what that is," says Pa. "Th' incubator is th' newfangled way o' cheatin' th' hens and raisin' chickens. I ain't so sure about th' breed o' chickens you mentioned."

"You've heard of germs, Mr. Sexton, haven't you?" says Professor Herbert.

"Jist call me Luster, if you don't mind," says Pa, very casual like.

"All right, Luster, you've heard of germs, haven't you?"

"Yes," says Pa, "but I don't believe in germs. I'm sixty-five years old and I ain't seen one yet!"

"You can't see them with your naked eye," says Professor Herbert. "Just keep that gun in the holster and stay with me in the high school today. I have a few things I want to show you. That scum on your teeth has germs in it."

"What," says Pa, "you mean to tell me I've got germs on my teeth!"

"Yes," says Professor Herbert. "The same kind as we might be able to find in a living black snake if we dissect it!"

"I don't mean to dispute your word," says Pa, "but I don't believe it. I don't believe I have germs on my teeth!"

"Stay with me today and I'll show you. I want to take you through the school anyway! School has changed a lot in the hills since you went to school. I don't guess we had high schools in this county when you went to school!"

"No," says Pa, "jist readin', writin', and cipherin'. We didn't have all this bug larnin', frog larnin', and findin' germs on your teeth and in the middle o' black snakes! Th' world's changin'."

"It is," says Professor Herbert, "and we hope all for the better. Boys like your own there are going to help change it. He's your boy. He knows all of what I've told you. You stay with me today."

"I'll shore stay with you," says Pa. "I want to see th' germs off'n my teeth. I jist want to see a germ. I've never seen one in my life. 'Seein' is believin',' Pap allus told me."

Pa walks out of the office with Professor Herbert. I just hoped Professor Herbert didn't have Pa arrested for pulling his gun. Pa's gun has always been a friend to him when he goes to settle disputes.

The bell rang. School took up. I saw the students when they marched in the schoolhouse look at Pa. They would grin and punch each other. Pa just stood and watched them pass in at the schoolhouse door.

When I went to my first class I saw Pa and Professor Herbert going around over the schoolhouse. I was in my geometry class when Pa and Professor Herbert came in the room. We were explaining our propositions on the blackboard. Professor Herbert and Pa just quietly came in and sat down for a while. The students in geometry looked at Pa. They must have wondered what he was doing in school. Before the class was over, Pa and Professor Herbert got up and went out. I saw them together down on the playground. Professor Herbert was explaining to Pa. I could see the prints of Pa's gun under his coat when he'd walk around.

At noon in the high school cafeteria Pa and Professor Herbert sat together at the little table where Professor Herbert always ate by himself. They ate together. The students watched the way Pa ate. He ate with his knife instead of his fork. A lot of the students felt sorry for me after they found out he was my father. They didn't have to feel sorry for me. I wasn't ashamed of Pa after I found out he wasn't going to shoot Professor Herbert. I was glad they had made friends. I wasn't ashamed of Pa. I wouldn't be as long as he behaved. He would find out about the high school as I had found out about the Lambert boys across the hill.

In the afternoon when we went to biology Pa was in the class. He was sitting on one of the high stools beside the microscope. We went ahead with our work just as if Pa wasn't in the class. I saw Pa take his knife and scrape tartar from one of his teeth. Professor Herbert put it on the lens and adjusted the microscope for Pa. He adjusted it and worked awhile. Then he says: "Now Luster, look! Put your eye right down to the light. Squint the other eye!"

Pa put his head down and did as Professor Herbert said. "I see 'im," says Pa. "Who'd a ever thought that? Right on a body's teeth! Right in a body's mouth. You're right certain they ain't no fake to this, Professor Herbert?"

"No, Luster," says Professor Herbert. "It's there. That's the germ. Germs live in a world we cannot see with the naked eye. We must use the microscope. There are millions of them in our bodies. Some are harmful. Others are helpful."

Pa holds his face down and looks through the microscope. We stop and watch Pa. He sits upon the tall stool. His knees are against the table. His legs are long. His coat slips up when he bends over. The handle of his gun shows. Professor Herbert pulls his coat down quickly.

"Oh, yes," says Pa. He gets up and pulls his coat down. Pa's face gets a little red. He knows about his gun and he knows he doesn't have any use for it in high school.

"We have a big black snake over here we caught yesterday," says Professor Herbert. "We'll chloroform him and dissect him and show you he has germs in his body, too."

"Don't do it," says Pa. "I believe you. I jist don't want to see you kill the black snake. I never kill one. They are good mousers and a lot o' help to us on the farm. I like black snakes. I jist hate to see people kill 'em. I don't allow 'em killed on my place."

The students look at Pa. They seem to like him better after he said that. Pa with a gun in his pocket but a tender heart beneath his ribs for snakes, but not for man! Pa won't whip a mule at home. He won't whip his cattle.

"Man can defend hisself," says Pa, "but cattle and mules can't. We have the drop on 'em. Ain't nothin' to a man that'll beat a good pullin' mule. He ain't got th' right kind o' a heart!"

Professor Herbert took Pa through the laboratory. He showed him the different kinds of work we were doing. He showed him our equipment. They stood and talked while we worked. Then they walked out together. They talked louder when they got out in the hall.

When our biology class was over I walked out of the room. It was our last class for the day. I would have to take my broom and sweep two hours to finish paying for the split cherry tree. I just wondered if Pa would want me to stay. He was standing in the hallway watching the students march out. He looked lost among us. He looked like a leaf turned brown on the tree among the treetop filled with growing leaves.

I got my broom and started to sweep. Professor Herbert walked up and says, "I'm going to let you do that some other time. You can go home with your father. He is waiting out there."

I laid my broom down, got my books, and went down the steps.

Pa says, "Ain't you got two hours o' sweepin' yet to do?"

I says, "Professor Herbert said I could do

it some other time. He said for me to go home with you."

"No," says Pa. "You are goin' to do as he says. He's a good man. School has changed from my day and time. I'm a dead leaf, Dave. I'm behind. I don't belong here. If he'll let me I'll get a broom and we'll both sweep one hour. That pays your debt. I'll hep you pay it. I'll ast 'im and see if he won't let me hep you."

"I'm going to cancel the debt," says Professor Herbert. "I just wanted you to understand, Luster."

"I understand," says Pa, "and since I understand, he must pay his debt fer th' tree and I'm goin' to hep 'im."

"Don't do that," says Professor Herbert. "It's all on me."

"We don't do things like that," says Pa, "we're just and honest people. We don't want somethin' fer nothin'. Professor Herbert, you're wrong now and I'm right. You'll haf to listen to me. I've larned a lot from you. My boy must go on. Th' world has left me. It changed while I've raised my family and plowed th' hills. I'm a just and honest man. I don't skip debts. I ain't larned 'em to do that. I ain't got much larnin' myself but I do know right from wrong atter I see through a thing."

Professor Herbert went home. Pa and I stayed and swept one hour. It looked funny to see Pa use a broom. He never used one at home. Mom used the broom. Pa used the plow. Pa did hard work. Pa says, "I can't sweep. Look at th' streaks o' dirt I leave on th' floor! Seems like no work a-tall fer me. Brooms is too light 'r somethin'. I'll jist do th' best I can, Dave. I've been wrong about th' school."

I says, "Did you know Professor Herbert can get a warrant out for you for bringing your pistol to school and showing it in his office! They can railroad you for that!"

"That's all made right," says Pa. "I've made that right. Professor Herbert ain't goin' to take it to court. He likes me. I like 'im. We jist had to get together. You must go on to school. I am as strong a man as ever come out'n th' hills fer my years and th' hard work I've done. But I'm behind, Dave. I'm a little man. Your hands will be softer than mine. Your clothes will be better. You'll allus look cleaner than your old Pap. Jist remember, Dave, to pay your debts and be honest. Jist be kind to animals and don't bother th' snakes. That's all I got agin th' school. Puttin' black snakes to sleep and cuttin' 'em open."

It was late when we got home. Stars were in the sky. The moon was up. The ground was frozen. Pa took his time going home. I couldn't run like I did the night before. It was ten o'clock before we got the work finished, our suppers eaten. Pa sat before the fire and told Mom he was going to take her and show her a germ sometime. Mom hadn't seen one either. Pa told her about the high school and the fine man Professor Herbert was. He told Mom about the strange school across the hill and how different it was from the school in their day and time.

TELL ABOUT THE STORY. The following questions help you check your reading comprehension. Put an *x* in the box next to each correct answer.

1. Dave was required to stay after school because he
   ☐ a. failed to hand in his homework.
   ☐ b. got into a fight with another student.
   ☐ c. had to earn a dollar by working.

2. At first, Dave was afraid that his father would
   ☐ a. force him to drop out of school.
   ☐ b. shoot Professor Herbert.
   ☐ c. give him many extra chores to do.

3. Luster Sexton didn't believe in germs because he
   ☐ a. had never seen any germs before.
   ☐ b. was in good health and had never been sick.
   ☐ c. had read that germs do not really exist.

4. At the end of the story, Professor Herbert said that he
   ☐ a. planned to take Luster to court.
   ☐ b. was angry with Dave for bringing his father to school.
   ☐ c. wanted to cancel the debt.

HANDLE NEW VOCABULARY WORDS. The following questions check your vocabulary skills. Put an *x* in the box next to each correct answer.

1. Professor Herbert thought that six dollars was a little steep for the cherry tree. As used here, the word *steep* means
   ☐ a. a sharp slope.
   ☐ b. much knowledge.
   ☐ c. too high a price.

2. Although Pa brought a gun to school, he was not afraid that Professor Herbert would get a warrant against him. Define the word *warrant*.
   ☐ a. a written order
   ☐ b. a letter to the editor
   ☐ c. a library book

3. Professor Herbert offered to dissect a snake to prove that it had germs in its body. Which expression best defines the word *dissect*?
   ☐ a. to frighten or scare
   ☐ b. to cut apart in order to examine
   ☐ c. to release or set free

4. Pa complained that students should be in school and should not gallivant all over the hills. The word *gallivant* means
   ☐ a. wander about idly.
   ☐ b. study seriously.
   ☐ c. read quickly.

☐ × 5 = ☐
NUMBER   YOUR
CORRECT   SCORE

☐ × 5 = ☐
NUMBER   YOUR
CORRECT   SCORE

63

IDENTIFY STORY ELEMENTS. The following questions check your knowledge of story elements. Put an *x* in the box next to each correct answer.

1. What is the *setting* of "Split Cherry Tree"?
   ☐ a. a college in a large city
   ☐ b. a country high school
   ☐ c. a laboratory in a hospital

2. Which of the following sentences illustrates *character development*?
   ☐ a. At the beginning of the story Pa was critical of Professor Herbert; at the end of the story Pa respected and admired him.
   ☐ b. At the beginning of the story Pa worked very hard; at the end of the story he decided to relax and enjoy life.
   ☐ c. At the beginning of the story Pa went to Dave's school; at the end of the story Pa told his wife about the visit.

3. Identify the statement that best expresses the *theme* of "Split Cherry Tree."
   ☐ a. The best way to settle differences is through a show of force.
   ☐ b. Education has remained pretty much the same over the years.
   ☐ c. Personal experience helps a father to appreciate how much school has changed since his day.

4. Pa and Professor Herbert resolved a *conflict* over
   ☐ a. the high cost of raising a family.
   ☐ b. the kind of clothes to wear to school.
   ☐ c. values and ideas in education.

☐ × 5 = ☐	
NUMBER CORRECT	YOUR SCORE

NOTE WORDS IN A PASSAGE. The following questions use the cloze technique to check your reading comprehension. Complete the paragraph by filling in each blank with one of the words listed below. Each word appears in the story. Since there are five words and four blanks, one of the words will not be used.

At one time or another, just about every schoolchild has heard the tale of George Washington and the _____(1) tree. Legend has it, of course, that Washington chopped down the tree and then _____(2) confessed to the deed. "Father, I cannot tell a _____(3)," he supposedly stated. That little story provides a useful moral, or _____(4), but there is absolutely no proof that the incident ever occurred.

later   lesson

professor

cherry   lie

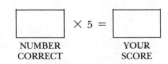

☐ × 5 = ☐	
NUMBER CORRECT	YOUR SCORE

KNOW HOW TO READ CRITICALLY. The following questions check your critical thinking skills. Put an *x* in the box next to each correct answer.

1. We may infer that the students who broke down the cherry tree were
   ☐ a. on their way home from school.
   ☐ b. away from school without permission.
   ☐ c. on a field trip.

2. It is fair to say that Pa's opinion of Professor Herbert
   ☐ a. did not change.
   ☐ b. changed after Pa met him.
   ☐ c. was not favorable at the end of the story.

3. Clues and hints in the story indicate that Pa
   ☐ a. had a very warm heart.
   ☐ b. was actually afraid of Professor Herbert.
   ☐ c. never told anyone about his day at school.

4. Which statement is true?
   ☐ a. Dave did not usually have much work to do at home after school.
   ☐ b. Professor Herbert did not treat Luster Sexton with respect.
   ☐ c. Visiting Dave's school proved to be an eye-opening experience for Luster.

Thinking for Writing and Discussion

- Although Luster Sexton and Professor Herbert were different in many ways, they were also very much alike. Do you agree or disagree with that statement? Offer evidence to support your answer.
- At the end of the story Pa told his son, "School has changed from my day and time. I'm a dead leaf, Dave." What did Pa mean by those words? Do you agree with him? Explain your answer.
- Sometimes a story offers a lesson, or moral. What lessons can be drawn from "Split Cherry Tree"? Present at least two.

Use the boxes below to total your scores for the exercises.

☐ **T**ELL ABOUT THE STORY
+
☐ **H**ANDLE NEW VOCABULARY WORDS
+
☐ **I**DENTIFY STORY ELEMENTS
+
☐ **N**OTE WORDS IN A PASSAGE
+
☐ **K**NOW HOW TO READ CRITICALLY
▼
☐ **Total Score:** Story 5

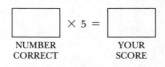

☐ × 5 = ☐

NUMBER   YOUR
CORRECT   SCORE

6. The Tiger's Heart

by Jim Kjelgaard

Meet the Author

Jim Kjelgaard (1910–1959) was born in New York City, but grew up on a farm in the mountains of Pennsylvania. There he developed the love of the outdoors that is reflected in his novels and short stories. *Forest Patrol*, Kjelgaard's first book, stemmed from his experiences as a forest ranger. Kjelgaard has also written several novels about animals. His most famous animal book is *Big Red*, the story of an Irish setter.

The approaching jungle night was a threat. As it grew darker, an eerie silence enveloped the village. People were silent. Cattle stood quietly. Chickens did not stir, and goats made no noise. Thus it had been for centuries, and thus it would continue to be. The inhabitants of the village knew the jungle. They were familiar with its narrow paths, its raging rivers, its steaming heat. They knew about its deer and crocodiles, its screaming green parrots, and countless other jungle creatures.

That was the daytime jungle they could see and feel and hear. But at night everything became different. When darkness came, the jungle was alive with strange and horrible things—things which no one had ever seen and no one could describe. There were shadows that had no substance, and one was unaware of them until they struck and killed. Then, when morning came, they changed themselves back into the shape of familiar things. Because the night was a time of the unknown, night had to be a time of fear.

Except, thought Pepe Garcia, except to the man who owned a rifle. As the night closed in, Pepe reached out to find his rifle, to make sure that it was close to him. As long as it was, he was king.

That was only fair, for the rifle had cost him dearly. With eleven others from his village, Pepe had gone to help chop a pathway for the new road. They used machetes, the indispensable long knife of all jungle dwellers, and they had worked hard. But unlike the rest, Pepe had saved every peso. With his savings, and through shrewd bargaining, he had bought his rifle, a supply of powder, lead, and bullets.

Many pesos the rifle had cost him. But it was worth the price. Though the jungle at night was fear itself, no man with a rifle had to fear. The others had only machetes with which to guard themselves from the terrors that came in the darkness. They were willing to pay—and pay well—for protection. So Pepe went peacefully to sleep.

He did not know what had awakened him, only that something was near. Pepe listened intently, but there was no change in the monotonous night sounds of the jungle. Still, something was not as it should be.

Then he heard it. At the far end of the village, near Juan Aria's hut, a goat bleated uneasily. Silence followed. The goat bleated again, louder and more fearful. There was a rush of small hoofs, a frightened bleat cut short, then silence again.

Because he owned a rifle, Pepe did not need to create fantastic and fearful creatures of the night. No, he had correctly interpreted what he had heard. A tiger, a jaguar, had come out in the night, had leaped the sharp fence which surrounded the village, and had made off with one of Juan Aria's goats.

Pepe went peacefully back to sleep. With morning, Juan Aria would certainly come to him.

Pepe did not awaken until the sun was up. Then he emerged from his hut, ate breakfast, and waited for the visitor he expected.

Presently Pepe saw two men, Juan Aria and his brother, coming up one of the paths that wound through the village. Other villagers stared, curious, but nobody else accompanied them because their flocks had not been raided. They had no wish to pay, or to help pay, a hunter.

Pepe waited until the two were near, and then said, "*Buenos días.*"[1]

"*Buenos días,*" they replied.

They sat down in the sun, looking at nothing in particular, not afraid any more, because the day was never a time of fear. By daylight, only now and again did a tiger come to raid a flock of goats, or kill a burro or a cow.

After a suitable lapse of time, Juan Aria said, "I brought my goats into the village last night, thinking they would be safe."

"And were they not?"

"They were not. Something came and killed one, a fine white-and-black nanny, my favorite. When the thing left, the goat went too. Never again shall I see her alive."

"What killed your goat?" Pepe inquired.

"This morning I saw only the tracks of a tiger."

"Did you hear it come?"

"I heard it."

"Then why did you not defend your flock?"

Juan Aria gestured with eloquent hands. "To attack a tiger with nothing but a machete would be madness."

---

1. **Buenos días:** Spanish for "Good day."

"That is true," Pepe agreed. "Let us hope that the next time it is hungry, this tiger will not come back for another goat."

"But it will!"

Pepe relaxed, for Juan Aria's admission greatly improved Pepe's bargaining position. And it was true that, having had a taste of easy game, the tiger would come again. Only death would end his forays, and since he knew where to find Juan Aria's goats, he would continue to attack them.

Pepe said, "That is bad, for a man may lose many goats to a tiger."

"Unless a hunter kills him," Juan Aria said.

"Unless a hunter kills him," Pepe agreed.

"That is why I have come to you, Pepe," Juan Aria said. A troubled frown spread over his face. "I hope you will follow and kill this tiger, for you are the only man who can do so."

"It would give me pleasure to kill him, but I cannot work for nothing."

"Nor do I expect you to. Even a tiger will not eat an entire goat, and you are sure to find what is left of my favorite nanny. Whatever the tiger has not eaten, you may have for your pay."

Pepe bristled. "You are saying that I should put myself and my rifle to work for the dead meat left by a tiger?"

"No, no!" Juan Aria protested. "In addition I will give you one live goat!"

"Three goats."

"I am a poor man!" the other wailed. "You would bankrupt me!"

"No man with twenty-nine goats is poor, though he may be if a tiger raids his flock a sufficient number of times," Pepe said.

"I will give you one goat!"

"Three goats!"

"You drive a hard bargain," Juan Aria said, "but I cannot deny you now. Kill the tiger."

Affecting an air of nonchalance, Pepe took his rifle from the fine blanket upon which it lay when he was not carrying it. He took his powder horn and bullet pouch, strapped his machete on, and sauntered toward Juan Aria's hut. A half-dozen children followed.

"Begone!" Pepe ordered.

They fell behind, but continued to follow until Pepe came to that place where Juan Aria's flock had passed the night. He glanced at the dust, and saw the tiger's great paw marks imprinted there. It was a huge cat, lame in the right front paw; it might have been injured in a battle with another tiger.

Expertly, Pepe located the place where it had gone over the sharp fence. Though the tiger had carried the sixty-pound goat in its jaws, it had cleared the fence at the place where it had leaped.

Though he did not look around, Pepe was aware of the villagers watching him, and he knew that their glances would be very respectful. From time to time men went into the jungle to work with their machetes, but no one would work where tigers were known to be. Not one would dare follow a tiger's trail. Only Pepe dared, and because he did, he must be respected and revered.

Walking slowly, as though without a care in the world, Pepe sauntered through the gate. Behind him he heard sighs of admiration and relief. A raiding tiger was a very real and terrible threat, and goats and cattle were not easily come by. The man with the rifle, the man able to protect them, must necessarily be a hero.

Once in the jungle and out of the villagers' sight, Pepe underwent a change. He shed his indifferent air and became serious and concerned. At once, he was as alert as a doe. A rifle might be a symbol of power, but unless a man was also a hunter, a rifle did him no good. Impressing the villagers was one thing; hunting a tiger was another.

Pepe knew the great cats could move with incredible swiftness and that they were strong enough to kill an ox. They feared nothing.

Wise in the ways of the jungle, Pepe slipped along as softly as a jungle shadow. As he moved, he glanced from time to time at the ground before him.

His trained eyes could detect a distinct trail. It consisted of an occasional drop of blood from the dead goat, a bent or broken plant, a few hairs where the tiger had squeezed between trees, and paw prints in soft places.

Within the first quarter of a mile Pepe knew many things about this tiger. He was not an ordinary beast, this tiger, or he would have gone a safe distance from the village, eaten what he wanted there, then covered the remainder of the goat with sticks and leaves. This tiger was not old, for his was not the lagging gait of an old cat, and the ease with which he had leaped the fence with a goat in his jaws was evidence of his strength.

Pepe stopped to check on the loading and priming of his rifle. There seemed to be nothing amiss, and there had better not be. When he saw the tiger, he must shoot straight and true. Warned by some jungle sense, Pepe slowed his pace. A moment later he found his game.

He came upon the tiger suddenly in a grove of scattered palm trees. Because he had not expected it there, Pepe did not see it until it was closer than safety allowed.

The tiger crouched at the base of a tree which was at least fifty feet high. Both of the beast's front paws were on what remained of the dead goat. The tiger did not snarl or grimace, or even twitch its tail. But there was a lethal, a deadly, quality about the great cat and an extreme tension. The tiger was bursting with raw anger that seemed to swell and grow.

Pepe stopped in his tracks, and cold fear crept up his spine. But he did not give way to fear. Very deliberately and carefully, he slowly brought the rifle to his shoulder and took aim. He had only one bullet and there would be no time to reload, but even a tiger could not withstand the smash of that shot between his eyes. Pepe steadied the rifle.

His finger tightened slowly on the trigger, for he must not let nervousness spoil his aim. When he pulled the trigger, Pepe's brain and body became numb for a moment.

There was no satisfying bang, no puff of black smoke wafting away from his muzzle. Instead there was only a sudden hiss, as though cold water had spilled on a hot stone. Pepe himself had loaded the rifle, but he could not have done it correctly.

Anger exploded in the tiger's deadly body. He let out a coughing snarl and launched his charge. Lord of the jungle, he would crush this puny man who dared to interfere with him!

In an instant, Pepe came back to reality. But he took time to think of his rifle, leaning it carefully against a tree while, in the same motion, he pulled his machete from its sheath.

It was now a hopeless fight, one which he knew would be decided in the tiger's favor, because not within the memory of the village's oldest inhabitant had any man ever killed a tiger with a machete. But he might as well fight helplessly as turn and run away, for if he did that he would surely be killed. No tiger that attacked anything was ever known to stop and turn away.

70

Machete in his hand, Pepe studied the onrushing cat. The tiger's right front foot was swollen to almost twice the size of the other. It must have stepped on a poisonous thorn or have been bitten by a snake.

Even with this handicap, a tiger was more than a match for a man armed with only a machete—but Pepe watched the right front paw carefully. If he had any advantage, it was there. Then the tiger, a terrible engine of destruction, flung himself at Pepe.

Pepe had known from the beginning that the tiger's first strike would be exactly like this, and he was ready for it. He swerved, bending his body outward as the great cat brushed past him. With all the strength in his powerful right arm, Pepe swung the machete. But he stopped his downward stroke just short of the tiger's back, for he suddenly knew that there was just one way to end this fight.

The tiger whirled and turned toward Pepe. Holding the machete before him like a sword, Pepe took a swift step backward. The tiger sprang, launching himself from the ground as though his rear legs were made of powerful steel springs. His flailing left paw flashed at Pepe. It hooked in his shirt, ripping it away as though it were paper. Burning claws sank into the flesh. Blood welled out.

Pepe did not try again to slash with the machete. Instead, he thrust, as he would have thrust with a knife or a sword. The machete's point met the tiger's throat, and Pepe put all of his strength and weight behind it. The tiger gasped.

The tiger pulled himself away. But blood was rushing from his throat now and he shook his head, then stumbled and fell. He pulled himself erect, looked with glazed eyes at Pepe, and dragged himself toward him. There was a low snarl and the tiger slumped to the ground. The tip of his tail twitched and was still.

Pepe stared, scarcely seeing the blood that flowed from his own wounded arm. He had done the impossible! He had killed a tiger with a machete! Pepe brushed a hand across his eyes and took a trembling step forward.

He picked up his rifle and looked at it closely. There seemed to be nothing wrong. Then, placing one foot against the tiger's head, he pulled the machete out.

Pepe held his rifle close to the machete wound. Then he pulled the trigger. The wound gaped wider, smoke blackening the fur around it. All traces of the machete wound were gone! For a moment Pepe felt the anguish of regret, and then braced himself, accepting it. For this was the way it must be.

In his village, everybody had a machete. In his village, the man who owned a rifle must remain supreme.

TELL ABOUT THE STORY. The following questions help you check your reading comprehension. Put an *x* in the box next to each correct answer.

1. The villagers counted on Pepe Garcia to hunt tigers because he
   - ☐ a. was the tallest and strongest man in the village.
   - ☐ b. enjoyed hunting tigers very much.
   - ☐ c. alone owned a rifle.

2. Pepe agreed to hunt the tiger in return for
   - ☐ a. the dead meat left by the tiger.
   - ☐ b. a goat.
   - ☐ c. three goats.

3. The tiger that Pepe was hunting
   - ☐ a. was very old.
   - ☐ b. had an injured front paw.
   - ☐ c. was not very strong.

4. Pepe killed the tiger by
   - ☐ a. stabbing it with his machete.
   - ☐ b. grabbing its throat and choking it.
   - ☐ c. shooting it with his rifle.

HANDLE NEW VOCABULARY WORDS. The following questions check your vocabulary skills. Put an *x* in the box next to each correct answer.

1. Because he dared to follow a tiger's trail, Pepe was respected and revered. What is the meaning of the word *revered*?
   - ☐ a. hated
   - ☐ b. ignored
   - ☐ c. greatly honored

2. Everyone used and depended on the machete—the indispensable long knife of all jungle dwellers. Define the word *indispensable*.
   - ☐ a. having little value; unimportant
   - ☐ b. absolutely essential; vital
   - ☐ c. dull or not sharp

3. Walking slowly, as though he didn't have a care in the world, Pepe sauntered through the gate. The word *sauntered* means
   - ☐ a. strolled.
   - ☐ b. dashed.
   - ☐ c. fell.

4. Pepe tried to make the villagers think he was indifferent about hunting the tiger, but he was actually serious and concerned. Which expression best defines the word *indifferent*?
   - ☐ a. not concerned
   - ☐ b. very worried
   - ☐ c. slightly injured

	× 5 =	
NUMBER CORRECT		YOUR SCORE

	× 5 =	
NUMBER CORRECT		YOUR SCORE

IDENTIFY STORY ELEMENTS. The following questions check your knowledge of story elements. Put an *x* in the box next to each correct answer.

1. What happened last in the *plot* of "The Tiger's Heart"?
   ☐ a. Juan Aria and his brother came to see Pepe.
   ☐ b. The tiger sprang at Pepe, ripping his shirt.
   ☐ c. Pepe saw the tiger's paw prints in the dust.

2. Which quotation *foreshadows* what will happen in the story?
   ☐ a. "Whatever the tiger has not eaten, you may have for your pay."
   ☐ b. "To attack a tiger with nothing but a machete would be madness."
   ☐ c. "That is bad, for a man may lose many goats to a tiger."

3. What was Pepe's *motive* for hunting the tiger?
   ☐ a. excitement
   ☐ b. revenge
   ☐ c. pay

4. In "The Tiger's Heart," the *conflict* is between
   ☐ a. Pepe and the villagers.
   ☐ b. Pepe and the tiger.
   ☐ c. Juan Aria and his brother.

☐ × 5 = ☐

NUMBER
CORRECT

YOUR
SCORE

NOTE WORDS IN A PASSAGE. The following questions use the cloze technique to check your reading comprehension. Complete the paragraph by filling in each blank with one of the words listed below. Each word appears in the story. Since there are five words and four blanks, one of the words will not be used.

Although the lion is called the "king of beasts," the tiger is even more powerful and more _____ . Large and 1
graceful, tigers possess great speed and incredible _____ . These 2
remarkable _____ can climb 3
trees and are capable of swimming many miles without becoming tired. All tigers are striped and brightly colored, and some grow to a length of fourteen feet. These tigers _____ more than the largest 4
lions.

accompanied   deadly

creatures

weigh   strength

☐ × 5 = ☐

NUMBER
CORRECT

YOUR
SCORE

73

KNOW HOW TO READ CRITICALLY. The following questions check your critical thinking skills. Put an *x* in the box next to each correct answer.

1. Why did Pepe shoot the tiger in the place where he had made the machete wound?
   - ☐ a. He wanted to make certain the tiger was dead.
   - ☐ b. He wanted to see if his rifle was still working.
   - ☐ c. He wanted to hide the machete wound.

2. Evidence in the story indicates that Pepe
   - ☐ a. had never tracked a tiger before.
   - ☐ b. was very skillful at tracking a tiger.
   - ☐ c. was a coward when he didn't have his rifle.

3. Which statement is true?
   - ☐ a. When his rifle failed to fire, Pepe was still confident that he would kill the tiger.
   - ☐ b. When his rifle failed to fire, Pepe thought that the tiger would kill him.
   - ☐ c. When his rifle failed to fire, Pepe thought that the best thing to do was to run away.

4. Why didn't Pepe reveal that he killed the tiger with a machete?
   - ☐ a. He was very modest and didn't want to boast.
   - ☐ b. He thought that nobody would believe him.
   - ☐ c. To do so would have decreased the importance of his valuable rifle.

<table>
<tr><td> </td><td>× 5 =</td><td> </td></tr>
<tr><td>NUMBER
CORRECT</td><td></td><td>YOUR
SCORE</td></tr>
</table>

Thinking for Writing and Discussion

- Pepe knew that "a rifle might be a symbol of power, but unless a man was also a hunter, a rifle did him no good." Present specific evidence to demonstrate that Pepe was an excellent hunter. If you wish, look back at the story.
- Suppose that Pepe told Juan Aria exactly how he killed the tiger. How do you think Juan would have reacted? What do you think Juan would have said?
- "The Tiger's Heart" contains many vivid descriptions. Examples include the silent village, the fierce tiger, and the violent battle. Suppose that Pepe returns to the village after killing the tiger. How do you think he describes the deadly fight? (Remember that Pepe cannot reveal that he used a machete.) Make your description as vivid as possible.

Use the boxes below to total your scores for the exercises.

☐ **T**ELL ABOUT THE STORY
+
☐ **H**ANDLE NEW VOCABULARY WORDS
+
☐ **I**DENTIFY STORY ELEMENTS
+
☐ **N**OTE WORDS IN A PASSAGE
+
☐ **K**NOW HOW TO READ CRITICALLY
▼
☐ **Total Score:** Story 6

7. The Revolt of Mother

by Mary E. Wilkins Freeman

Meet the Author

Mary E. Wilkins Freeman (1852–1930) is noted for her realistic stories about New England life. Freeman spent the first fifty years of her life in her home state, Massachusetts, and in Vermont. As a result, her fiction presents a very accurate picture of that region. Freeman wrote more than 225 stories, 12 novels, and a play. "The Revolt of Mother" and "A New England Nun" are her best-known short stories.

"Father!"

"What is it?"

"What are them men diggin' over there in the field for?"

The lower part of the old man's face suddenly dropped, as if some heavy weight had settled there. He shut his mouth tight and went on putting the harness on the mare. He fastened the collar on to her neck with a pull.

"Father!"

The old man slapped the saddle on the mare's back.

"Look here, father, I want to know what them men are diggin' over in the field for, and I'm goin' to know."

"I wish you'd go into the house, mother, and 'tend to your own affairs," the old man said. He ran his words together, and his speech was as difficult to understand as a growl.

But the woman understood his words. "I ain't goin' into the house till you tell me what them men are doin' over there in the field."

Then she stood waiting. She was a small woman, gray haired, wearing a brown cotton dress. Her name was Sarah Penn; her husband's name was Adoniram, though she always called him *father,* and he addressed her as *mother.*

They were in the barn, standing in front of the wide open doors. The spring air, full of the smell of growing grass and unseen blossoms, drifted in. The yard in front was littered with farm wagons and piles of wood. On the sides, close to the fence and the house, the grass was a vivid green, and there were some dandelions.

The old man glanced doggedly, stubbornly, at his wife as he tightened the last buckles on the harness. She looked firm in her purpose, unmoving, solid as a rock. He slapped the reins on the horse and started out from the barn.

"Father!" she said.

The old man pulled up the horse. "What is it?"

"I want to know what them men are diggin' over there in that field for."

"They're diggin' a cellar, I suppose, if you've got to know."

"A cellar for what?"

"A barn."

"A barn? You ain't goin' to build a barn over there where we was goin' to have a house?"

The old man said not another word. He shook the reins and hurried the horse out of the yard.

The woman stood a moment looking at him, and then she went out of the barn across a corner of the yard to the house. The house stood at right angles to the great barn and a long stretch of huge farm sheds. The house was so small as to be infinitesimal compared with them.

A pretty girl was looking out one of the house windows. She was watching three men who were digging over in the field which bounded the yard near the road line. She turned quietly when the woman entered.

"What are they diggin' for, mother?" she said. "Did he tell you?"

"They're diggin' for—a cellar for a new barn."

"Oh, mother, he ain't going to build another barn?"

"That's what he says."

A boy stood in front of the kitchen mirror combing his hair. He combed slowly and painstakingly, arranging his brown hair over his forehead. He did not seem to pay any attention to the conversation.

"Sammy," asked the girl, "did you know father was going to build a new barn?"

The boy kept combing with great care.

"Sammy!"

He turned, showing a face which looked remarkably like his father's.

"Yes, I suppose I did," he said, reluctantly.

"How long have you known it?" asked his mother.

"About three months, I guess."

"Why didn't you tell me?"

"Didn't think it would do no good."

"I don't see what father wants another barn for," said the girl, in a low voice. She turned again to the window, and stared out at the digging men in the field, her face full of distress.

Her mother looked sternly at the boy. "Is he goin' to buy more cows?" she said.

The boy did not reply; he was tying his shoes.

"Sammy, I want you to tell me if he's goin' to buy more cows."

"I suppose he is."

"How many?"

"Four, I guess."

His mother said nothing more. The boy got his cap from a nail behind the door, took an old arithmetic book from the shelf, and started for school.

The girl went to the sink and began to wash the dishes that were piled up there. Her mother came to her side and said, "You wipe 'em, I'll wash. There's a good many this morning."

"Mother," said the girl, "don't you think it's too bad father's going to build that new barn, much as we need a decent house to live in?"

Her mother scrubbed a dish fiercely. "You ain't found out yet we're women-folks, Nanny Penn," she said. "You ain't seen enough of men-folks yet to know. One of these days you'll find it out."

After several moments of silence, Sarah Penn spoke again. "You hadn't ought to judge father, though," she said. "He can't help it 'cause he don't look at things just the way we do. And we've been pretty comfortable here, after all."

Sarah Penn finished washing the pans and then swept the small box of a house. Afterwards, she got out a mixing bowl and a board, and made some dough for pies.

"We must have the stove moved out into the shed before too long," thought Mrs. Penn, as she worked. "Talk about not having enough room, it's been a real blessing to be able to put the stove in the shed in hot weather."

Sarah Penn was making mince pies. Her husband, Adoniram Penn, liked them better than any other kind. She hurried this morning, since it had been later than usual when she began, and she wanted to have a pie baked for dinner. However deep an anger or resentment she might be forced to hold against her husband, she would never fail to attend to his needs. So she made the pies carefully, while across the table she could see, when she glanced out the window, the sight that rankled, that pained her patient and steadfast soul— the digging of the cellar of the new barn in the place where Adoniram forty years ago had promised her their new house should stand.

Adoniram and Sammy returned for lunch a few minutes after noon. They ate promptly and then rose up and went about their work. Sammy went back to school, while Adoniram went to work in the yard unloading wood from the wagon. Sarah put away the dishes while Nanny left to go to the store.

When Nanny was gone, Mrs. Penn went to the door. "Father!" she called.

"Well, what is it?" he replied.

"I want to see you for just a minute, father."

"I can't leave this wood nohow. I've got to get it unloaded and go for a load of gravel before two o'clock."

"I want to see you just a minute."

"I tell you I can't stop nohow, now."

"Father, you come here." Sarah Penn stood in the doorway like a queen. She held her head high, as though it carried a crown; there was in her that patience which made authority royal in her voice. Adoniram went.

Mrs. Penn led the way into the kitchen, and pointed to a chair. "Sit down, father," she said. "I've got something I want to say to you."

He sat down heavily. His face was quite stolid and he showed no emotion, but he looked at her with uneasy eyes. "Well, what is it, mother?"

"I want to know what you're buildin' that new barn for, father."

"I ain't got nothin' to say about it."

"It can't be you think you need another barn?"

"I tell you I ain't got nothin' to say about it, mother; and I ain't goin' to say nothin'."

"Are you goin' to buy more cows?"

Adoniram did not reply; he shut his mouth tight.

"I know you are. Now, father, look here," said Sarah Penn, "I'm goin' to talk real plain to you; I never have since I married you, but

I'm goin' to now. I ain't never complained, and I ain't goin' to complain now, but I'm goin' to talk plain. You see this room here, father. You look at it well. You see there ain't no carpet on the floor, and you see the paper is all dirty, and droppin' off the walls. We ain't had no new paper on it for ten years, and then I put it on myself, and it didn't cost but pennies a roll.

"You see this room, father. It's all the one I've had to work in and eat in and sit in since we were married. It's all the room our Nanny's got for company, and all her friends have better than this, and their fathers don't have half the means that you have. It's the room she'll have to be married in! We were married in my mother's parlor, with a carpet on the floor, and stuffed furniture, and a mahogany table. And this is all the room my daughter will have to be married in! Look here, father!"

Sarah Penn marched across the room. She flung open a door and disclosed a tiny bedroom, only large enough for a bed and a dresser.

"There, father," she said, "there's all the room I've had to sleep in for forty years. All my children were born there—the two that died, and the two that's livin'. I was sick with a fever there."

She threw open another door. A narrow, crooked flight of stairs wound upward from it. "There, father," she said, "I want you to look at those two unfinished rooms that are all the places our son and daughter have had to sleep in all their lives. Those are the places they have to sleep in. They ain't as good as your horse's stall. They ain't as warm and tight."

Sarah Penn went back and stood in front of her husband. "Now, father," she said, "I want to know if you think you're doin' right accordin' to what you said. Here, when we were married forty years ago, you promised me faithful that we should have a new house built in that lot over in the field before the year was out. You said you had money enough, and you wouldn't ask me to live in no such place as this. It is forty years now, and you've been makin' more money, and I've been savin' of it, and you ain't built no house yet. You've built sheds and cowhouses and one new barn. And now you're goin' to build another. Father, I want to know if you think it's right. You're lodgin' your dumb beasts better than you are your own flesh and blood. I want to know if you think it's right."

"I ain't got nothin' to say."

"You can't say nothin' without ownin' it ain't right, father."

Mrs. Penn's face was burning; her eyes gleamed. She had pleaded her case like a Webster;[1] but Adoniram remained silent.

"Father, ain't you got nothin' to say?" said Mrs. Penn.

"I've got to get that load of gravel. I can't stand here talkin' all day."

"Father, won't you think it over, and have a house built there instead of a barn?"

But Adoniram kept to his obstinate, stubborn silence.

"I ain't got nothin' to say."

All through spring it seemed to Sarah Penn that she heard nothing but the noises of saws and hammers. The new barn grew fast. It was a fine building for this little village. People came on Sundays when the weather was good and stood around, admiring it. Mrs. Penn did not speak of it, and Adoniram did not mention it to her.

---

1. **Daniel Webster:** an American politician and lawyer known for his powerful speeches.

The barn was completed and ready for use by the third week in July. Adoniram had planned to move his cows in on Wednesday. On Tuesday he received a letter which changed his plans. He came in with it early in the morning.

"Sammy's been to the post office," said Adoniram. "And I've got this letter from Hiram." Hiram was Mrs. Penn's brother who lived in Vermont.

"Well," said Mrs. Penn, "what does he say about the folks?"

"I guess they're all right. He says if I come up there right now there's a chance to buy just the kind of horse I want." He stared thoughtfully out the window at the new barn.

"I don't know but what I'd better go," said Adoniram. "I hate to go off just now, right in the midst of hayin', but the ten-acre lot's cut, and I guess the others can get along without me three or four days. I can't get a horse round here to suit me, nohow, and I've got to have another for all that wood haulin' in the fall. I told Hiram to watch out, and if he got wind of a good horse to let me know. I guess I'd better go."

"I'll get out your clean shirt and collar," said Mrs. Penn, calmly.

When he was all ready with his coat and hat brushed, and a lunch packed in a paper bag, he hesitated at the door. He looked at his wife, and said softly, "*If* them cows come tomorrow, Sammy can drive 'em into the new barn, and when they bring the hay up later, they can pitch it in there."

When he was just over the door step, Adoniram turned and looked back, as though somehow nervous. "I shall be back by Saturday," he said.

"Do be careful," replied his wife.

She stood in the door with Nanny at her elbow and watched him out of sight. Her eyes had a strange expression in them.

All that morning Mrs. Penn seemed to be deep in thought. "Suppose I *had* wrote to Hiram," she once muttered out loud. "Suppose I *had* wrote and asked him if he knew of any horse. But I *didn't* write, and father's going there wasn't none of my doin'. Funny that letter from Hiram should come just today. It looks like a sign."

She said the last words out so loud that Nanny overheard her and called out, "What are you talking about, mother?"

"Nothin'," said Mrs. Penn. But she kept thinking about the letter. And finally she made up her mind as to her course of action.

At eleven o'clock the load of hay from the west field came up. They were taking it over to the new barn. Mrs. Penn ran out. "Stop!" she called, "stop!"

The men stopped and looked. From the top of the load, Sammy stared at his mother.

"Stop!" she cried out again. "Don't you put the hay in that barn; put it in the old one."

"Why, he said to put it in here," replied one of the workers, surprised. He was a young man, a neighbor's son, whom Adoniram hired by the year to help on the farm.

"Don't put the hay in the new barn; there's room enough in the old barn, ain't there?" said Mrs. Penn.

"There's room enough," said the hired man. "Didn't need the new barn, nohow, as far as room's concerned. Well, I suppose he changed his mind." He took hold of the reins and turned the horse around.

Mrs. Penn went back to the house. Nanny came up to her side and said, wonderingly, "I thought father wanted them to put the hay into the new barn."

"It's all right," replied her mother.

Sammy slid down from the load of hay

and came in to see if lunch was ready.

Mrs. Penn set out the food on the kitchen table. "You'd better eat your lunch now," she said. "I want you to help me afterward."

Nanny and Sammy stared at each other. There was something strange in their mother's voice and manner. Mrs. Penn did not eat anything herself. She went into the pantry, and they heard her moving dishes while they ate. After a while she came out with a pile of plates. She got the clothes basket out of the shed, and packed them into it. Nanny and Sammy watched. She brought out cups and saucers and put them in with the plates.

"What are you going to do, mother?" asked Nanny in a timid voice.

"You'll see what I'm goin' to do," replied Mrs. Penn. "If you're through, Nanny, I want you to go upstairs and pack up your things; and I want you, Sammy, to help me take down the bed in the bedroom."

"Mother, what for?" gasped Nanny.

"You'll see."

It was an amazing feat that was performed over the next few hours. The family, with Sarah Penn in charge, moved all their household goods into the new barn. By five o'clock in the afternoon the little house in which the Penns had lived for forty years had been completely emptied into the new barn.

Sarah Penn walked about the new barn, pleased at the possibilities she saw. Those large stalls would make fine bedrooms, better bedrooms than the one she had occupied for forty years. The harness room, with its chimney and shelves, would make the kitchen of her dreams. The middle space would be a parlor, with a little work, fit for a palace. Upstairs there was as much room as down. With walls and windows, what a house there would be!

At six o'clock the stove was going in the harness room, the kettle was boiling, and the table was set for tea. It looked almost as homelike there as the abandoned house across the yard ever had.

When the hired man came later to drop off the pails of milk, Sarah calmly directed him to bring the milk to the new barn. He came in, looked around, gaping, amazed. Before the next morning he had spread all over the village the story of Adoniram Penn's wife moving into the new barn. Everywhere people stopped to discuss it; anything out of the ordinary in this quiet town made people talk. There was a difference of opinion with regard to Sarah. Some considered her crazy; some thought her wild.

On Friday the minister went to see her. They spoke for a while.

Finally, she said, "There ain't no use talkin', Mr. Hersey. I've thought it all over and over, and I believe I'm doin' what's right."

"Well, of course, if you feel satisfied that you are doing right," said the minister, helplessly. Privately, he was wondering how Adoniram Penn would deal with his wife. In fact, everybody in the village wondered.

When Adoniram's four new cows arrived, Sarah ordered three to be put in the barn, the other in the shed where the stove had stood. The villagers talked about that, too. Meanwhile, the family waited for Adoniram.

Toward evening on Saturday, when Adoniram was expected back, Sarah Penn had supper all ready. Nanny and Sammy kept close at her heels. They felt a bit nervous.

Sammy looked out the window of the new barn. "There he is," he announced. Mrs. Penn went on about her work. The children watched Adoniram leave the new horse standing in the drive while he went to the door of the house. It was locked. Then he went around to the shed. That door was never locked, even when the family was away. Nanny anxiously wondered how her father would react when he saw the new cow there. Adoniram emerged from the shed and stood looking around in a dazed manner. His lips moved; he was saying something, but they could not hear what it was. The hired man was peeping around a corner of the old barn, but nobody saw him.

Adoniram took the new horse by the bridle and led him across the yard to the new barn. The barn doors rolled open, and there stood his family.

Adoniram stared at the group. "What on earth are you all down here for?" he said. "What's the matter over at the house?"

"We've come here to live, father," said Sammy. His thin voice trembled bravely.

"What"—Adoniram sniffed—"what is it, smells like cookin'?" he said. He stepped forward and looked into the new barn. Then he turned to his wife. His old face was pale and frightened. "What on earth does this mean, mother?" he gasped.

"You come in here, father," said Sarah. She led the way and shut the door. "Now, father," said she, "you needn't be scared. I ain't crazy. There ain't nothin' to be upset over. But we've come here to live, and we're goin' to live here. We've got just as good a right here as new horses and cows. The house wasn't fit for us to live in any longer, and I made up my mind I wasn't goin' to stay there. I've done my duty by you for forty years, and I'm goin' to do it now; but I'm goin' to live here. You've got to put in some windows and walls; and you'll have to buy some furniture."

"Why, mother!" the old man gasped.

"You'd better take your coat off and get washed. There's the wash basin—and then we'll have supper."

"Why, mother!"

Outside, Sammy went past the window, leading the new horse to the old barn. The old man saw him, and shook his head speechlessly. He tried to take off his coat, but his arms seemed to lack the power. His wife helped him. She poured some water into the tin basin, and put in a piece of soap. Then she put the food on the table. Sammy came in, and the family drew up. Adoniram sat dazed, looking at his plate, and they waited.

"Ain't you goin' to ask a blessing, father?" said Sarah.

The old man bent his head and mumbled.

All through the meal he paused to stop eating, and stared at his wife. He was shocked, but the food tasted good, and he ate well. After supper he went out and sat down on the steps of the new barn, the barn in which he had planned to keep his cows, but which Sarah had converted to a house.

After the supper dishes were cleared away and everything was cleaned, Sarah joined him. The twilight was deepening. There was a clear green glow in the sky. Before them stretched the fields. In the distance they could see haystacks, tall, like the huts of a village. The air was calm and sweet.

Sarah bent over and touched her husband on one of his thin, sinewy shoulders.

"Father!"

The old man's shoulders moved. He was weeping.

"Why, don't do that, father," said Sarah.

"I'll—put in the—walls—windows—everything you want."

Sarah touched her apron up to her eyes; she was overcome by her own triumph.

Adoniram was like a fortress whose walls had come tumbling down.

"Why, mother," he said hoarsely, "I hadn't no idea this meant so much to you."

TELL ABOUT THE STORY. The following questions help you check your reading comprehension. Put an *x* in the box next to each correct answer.

1. Sarah Penn became upset when she discovered that her husband was
   - ☐ a. planning to buy a new horse.
   - ☐ b. going to spend several days in Vermont.
   - ☐ c. building a new barn.

2. Adoniram and Sarah had lived together in the house for
   - ☐ a. about a year.
   - ☐ b. nearly twenty years.
   - ☐ c. forty years.

3. When the villagers learned that Sarah had moved her family into the new barn, they
   - ☐ a. approved of her actions.
   - ☐ b. considered her wild and foolish.
   - ☐ c. believed that Adoniram would be pleased.

4. At the conclusion of "The Revolt of Mother," Adoniram
   - ☐ a. gave in to his wife completely.
   - ☐ b. insisted that the family move back into the old house.
   - ☐ c. rushed away in a fit of anger.

HANDLE NEW VOCABULARY WORDS. The following questions check your vocabulary skills. Put an *x* in the box next to each correct answer.

1. Adoniram was shocked to discover that Sarah had converted the new barn to a house. The word *converted* means
   - ☐ a. changed.
   - ☐ b. destroyed.
   - ☐ c. paid for.

2. Sarah Penn flung open the door and disclosed a tiny bedroom just big enough for a bed and a dresser. What is the meaning of the word *disclosed*?
   - ☐ a. painted
   - ☐ b. surprised
   - ☐ c. revealed

3. When Sarah Penn looked out the window and saw the new barn, the sight rankled and pained her. The word *rankled* means
   - ☐ a. pleased.
   - ☐ b. angered.
   - ☐ c. encouraged.

4. Compared to the great barn and the long stretch of huge farm sheds, the house was so small as to be infinitesimal. Define the word *infinitesimal*.
   - ☐ a. enormous
   - ☐ b. tiny
   - ☐ c. colorful

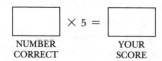

	× 5 =	
NUMBER CORRECT		YOUR SCORE

	× 5 =	
NUMBER CORRECT		YOUR SCORE

IDENTIFY STORY ELEMENTS. The following questions check your knowledge of story elements. Put an *x* in the box next to each correct answer.

1. What happened last in the *plot* of the story?
   □ a. The men began digging a cellar for the barn.
   □ b. Adoniram left to see Mrs. Penn's brother.
   □ c. Mrs. Penn and her children moved into the new barn.

2. Which pair of words best *characterizes* Sarah Penn?
   □ a. selfish, greedy
   □ b. earnest, determined
   □ c. thoughtless, wasteful

3. "You're lodgin' your dumb beasts better than you are your own flesh and blood." That line of *dialogue* was spoken by
   □ a. Sarah.
   □ b. Adoniram.
   □ c. the minister.

4. In addition to the main conflict between Sarah and Adoniram, Sarah experiences *inner conflict* when she
   □ a. thought about the letter all morning and finally made up her mind.
   □ b. told the men to put the hay into the old barn.
   □ c. had a discussion with the preacher.

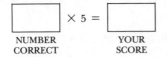

NUMBER CORRECT   YOUR SCORE

NOTE WORDS IN A PASSAGE. The following questions use the cloze technique to check your reading comprehension. Complete the paragraph by filling in each blank with one of the words listed below. Each word appears in the story. Since there are five words and four blanks, one of the words will not be used.

Daniel Webster was probably the most able and respected lawyer of his time. An _____ on government, he served for fifteen years in the United States Senate. Webster's claim to fame, however, rested on his truly _____ speeches. Fiery and forceful, they thrilled his audiences and filled them with _____. Teachers often asked their students to memorize and recite Webster's powerful _____.

authority   nervous

emotion

amazing   words

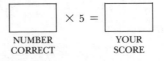

NUMBER CORRECT   YOUR SCORE

KNOW HOW TO READ CRITICALLY. The following questions check your critical thinking skills. Put an *x* in the box next to each correct answer.

1. The title of the story suggests that a character will
   - ☐ a. challenge something or somebody.
   - ☐ b. go along with what others think.
   - ☐ c. accept being ignored.

2. What helped Sarah take her course of action?
   - ☐ a. the opinion of the villagers
   - ☐ b. a suggestion made by Sammy
   - ☐ c. the letter from Hiram, which she interpreted as a sign

3. Which statement is true?
   - ☐ a. The minister finally convinced Sarah to move back into the old house.
   - ☐ b. Adoniram needed a new barn because he didn't have enough space for his cows.
   - ☐ c. Adoniram hadn't realized how important a new house was to Sarah.

4. At the conclusion of "The Revolt of Mother," Sarah was
   - ☐ a. quite angry.
   - ☐ b. very unhappy.
   - ☐ c. pleased and moved.

☐ × 5 = ☐

NUMBER   YOUR
CORRECT   SCORE

Thinking for Writing and Discussion

- When "The Revolt of Mother" first appeared many years ago, it created a sensation because of Sarah Penn's actions. Why do you think people in those days reacted as they did? How do you think most people today view Sarah's actions? Explain your answers.
- Suppose Hiram had not sent the letter. How do you think the story would have ended? If you believe it would have ended the same way, give reasons to support your opinion.
- At the end of the story, Adoniram Penn is pictured as "a fortress whose walls had come tumbling down." Why do you think the author used that image to describe Adoniram? How accurate is it? Why?

Use the boxes below to total your scores for the exercises.

☐ **T**ELL ABOUT THE STORY
+
☐ **H**ANDLE NEW VOCABULARY WORDS
+
☐ **I**DENTIFY STORY ELEMENTS
+
☐ **N**OTE WORDS IN A PASSAGE
+
☐ **K**NOW HOW TO READ CRITICALLY
▼
☐ **Total Score:** Story 7

8. The Story-Teller

by Saki

*I*t was a hot afternoon and the railroad car was stifling. The next stop was Templecombe, nearly an hour ahead. The occupants of the car were a small girl, a smaller girl, and a small boy. An aunt belonging to the children occupied one corner seat, and the corner seat on the opposite side was occupied by a young man who was a stranger to their party. The aunt and the children spoke to each other in a limited, persistent way. Most of the aunt's remarks seemed to begin with "*Don't!*" and nearly all of the children's remarks began with "*Why?*" The young man said nothing.

"Don't, Cyril, *don't!*" exclaimed the aunt, as the small boy began whacking the cushions of the seat, producing a cloud of dust at each blow.

"Come and look out the window," she added.

The child moved reluctantly to the window. "Why are those sheep being led out of that field?" he asked.

"I guess they are being led to another field where there is more grass," the aunt said weakly.

Meet the Author

Saki (1870–1916) is the pen name of H. H. Munro, a writer famous for his witty and amusing short stories. Born in Burma, he was sent to England to live with his two aunts when his mother died. Saki eventually moved to London where he worked as a journalist and wrote stories in his spare time. It is said that the aunt in "The Story-Teller" is based on his Aunt Charlotte, who brought him up very strictly.

"But there is lots of grass in that field," protested the boy. "There's nothing else but grass there, Aunt. There's *lots* of grass in that field."

"Perhaps the grass in the other field is better," suggested the aunt a bit foolishly.

"Why is it better?" came the swift, obvious, and inevitable question.

"Oh, look at those cows!" exclaimed the aunt. Nearly every field along the way had contained some cows, but she spoke as though she were drawing attention to a rarity, something unusual.

"Why is the grass in the other field better?" persisted Cyril.

The frown on the young man's face was changing to a scowl. The aunt looked at him and decided that he was a very unfeeling and unsympathetic man. She was unable to come to any satisfactory decision about the grass in the other field.

The smaller girl made a nuisance of herself by beginning to recite "On the Road to Mandalay." She knew only the first line of the poem, but she put her knowledge of it to the fullest use. Over and over and over again, she repeated the line in a dreamy, but firm and very audible voice. It seemed to the young man as though someone had made a bet with her that she could not repeat that line out loud two thousand times without stopping. Whoever it was who had made that wager was sure to lose the bet.

"Come over here and listen to a story," said the aunt, when the young man had looked twice at her with annoyance.

The children moved slowly and listlessly toward the aunt's end of the railroad car. Evidently her reputation as a story-teller did not rank high in their opinion.

In a low voice, interrupted at frequent intervals by loud, impatient questions from the children, she began an extremely boring story about a little girl who was good, and was finally saved from an angry bull by a number of rescuers who were happy to help her because she was so good.

"Wouldn't they have saved her if she hadn't been good?" asked the bigger of the small girls. It was exactly the question that the young man had wanted to ask.

"Well, yes," admitted the aunt, lamely. "But I don't think they would have run quite so fast to help her if they had not liked her so much."

"It's the stupidest story I ever heard," said the bigger of the small girls with immense conviction.

"I didn't listen after the first bit, it was so stupid," said Cyril.

The smaller girl made no actual comment on the story. She just kept repeating over and over the same line of poetry she had been saying before.

"You don't seem to be very successful as a story-teller," said the young man suddenly from the corner.

The aunt bristled instant defense at this unexpected attack.

"It's a very difficult thing to tell stories that children can both understand and appreciate," she said stiffly.

"I don't agree with you," said the young man.

"Perhaps *you* would like to tell them a story" was the aunt's retort.

"Yes, tell us a story," demanded the bigger of the small girls.

"Once upon a time," began the young man, "there was a little girl named Bertha, who was extraordinarily good."

The children's interest began at once to flicker; all stories seemed dreadfully alike, no matter who told them.

"She did all that she was told, she was always

truthful, she kept her clothes clean, ate properly, learned her lessons perfectly, and was polite in her manners."

"Was she pretty?" asked the bigger of the small girls.

"Not as pretty as any of you," said the young man, "but she was horribly good."

There was a wave of reaction in favor of the story. The word *horrible* in connection with the word *good* was a novelty—something new that appealed to the children. It seemed to introduce a ring of truth that was absent from all of the aunt's tales.

"She was so good," continued the young man, "that she won several medals for goodness. These she always wore pinned to her dress. There was a medal for obedience. There was another for punctuality. And there was a third for good behavior. They were large metal medals, and they clinked against one another as she walked. No other child in the town where she lived had as many as three medals, so everybody knew that she must be an extra good child."

"Horribly good," quoted Cyril.

"Everybody talked about her goodness," continued the young man, "and the Prince of the country got to hear about it, and he said that as she was so very good she might be allowed once a week to walk in his park, which was just outside the town. It was a beautiful park, and no children were ever allowed in it, so it was a great honor for Bertha to be allowed to go there."

"Were there any sheep in the park?" demanded Cyril.

"No," said the young man, "there were no sheep."

"Why weren't there any sheep?" came the obvious question.

The aunt permitted herself a smile, which might almost have been described as a grin.

"There were no sheep in the park," said the young man, "because the Prince's mother had once had a dream that her son would either be killed by a sheep or else by a clock falling on him. For that reason the Prince never kept a sheep in his park or a clock in his palace."

The aunt managed to hold back and suppress a gasp of admiration.

"Was the Prince killed by a sheep or by a clock?" asked Cyril.

"He is still alive, so we can't tell whether the dream will come true," said the young man, easily. "Anyway, there were no sheep in the park, but there were lots of little pigs running all over the place."

"What color were they?"

"Black with white faces, white with black spots, black all over, gray with white patches, and some were white all over."

The story-teller paused to let a full picture of the park's pigs sink into the children's imaginations. Then he resumed.

"Bertha was rather sorry to discover that there were no flowers in the park. She had promised her aunt, with tears in her eyes, that she would not pick any of the kind Prince's flowers, and she had meant to keep her promise, so of course it made her feel silly to find out that there were no flowers to pick."

"Why weren't there any flowers?"

"Because the pigs had eaten them all," said the young man promptly. "The gardener had told the Prince that you couldn't have pigs and flowers, so he decided to have pigs and no flowers."

There was a murmur of approval at the excellent decision the Prince had made. So many people would have decided the other way.

"There were lots of other delightful things

in the park. There were ponds with gold and blue and green fish in them, and trees with beautiful parrots that said clever things at a moment's notice, and hummingbirds that hummed all the popular tunes of the day. Bertha walked up and down and enjoyed herself immensely. She thought to herself: 'If I were not so extraordinarily good, I would not have been allowed to come into this beautiful park to enjoy all that there is to be seen in it.' And her three medals clinked against one another as she walked and helped to remind her how very good she really was. Just then an enormous wolf came prowling into the park to see if it could catch a fat little pig for its supper."

"What color was it?" asked the children, with an immediate quickening of interest.

"Mud color all over, with a black tongue and pale gray eyes that gleamed fiercely. The first thing that it saw in the park was Bertha. Her clothing was so spotlessly white and clean that it could be seen from a great distance. Bertha saw the wolf and saw that it was creeping toward her, and she began to wish that she had never been allowed to come into the park. She ran as hard as she could, and the wolf came after her with huge leaps and bounds. She managed to reach a thick grove of bushes, and she hid herself in one of the thickest bushes.

"The wolf came sniffing among the branches, its black tongue lolling out of its mouth and its pale gray eyes glaring with rage. Bertha was terribly frightened, and she thought to herself: 'If I had not been so extraordinarily good, I would have been safe in the town at this moment.' However, the scent of the bushes was very strong, so that the wolf could not sniff out where Bertha was hiding. And the bushes were so thick that he might have hunted about in them for a long time without catching sight of her, so he thought he might as well go off and catch a little pig instead. Bertha was trembling very much at having the wolf so near her, and as she trembled the medal for obedience clinked against the medals for good behavior and punctuality. The wolf was just moving away when he heard the sound of the medals clinking. He stopped to listen. They clinked again somewhere in a bush quite near him. He dashed into the bush, his pale gray eyes gleaming with triumph, and dragged Bertha out and devoured her to the last morsel. All that was left of her were her shoes, bits of clothing, and the three medals for goodness."

"Were any of the little pigs killed?"

"No, they all escaped."

"The story began badly," said the smaller of the girls. "But it had a beautiful ending."

"It is the most beautiful story that I ever heard," said the bigger of the small girls, decisively.

"It is the *only* beautiful story I have ever heard," said Cyril.

A very different opinion came from the aunt.

"That is a *very* incorrect—a very improper—story to tell to young children! You have very nearly ruined the effect of years of careful teaching."

"At any rate," said the young man, collecting his luggage and getting ready to leave the car, "I kept them quiet for ten minutes, which was more than you were able to do."

"Poor aunt," he thought to himself as he walked down the platform of Templecombe station. "For the next six months or so, those children will demand, in public, that she tell them an improper story."

TELL ABOUT THE STORY. The following questions help you check your reading comprehension. Put an *x* in the box next to each correct answer.

1. The children thought that the aunt's story was
   - ☐ a. stupid.
   - ☐ b. believable.
   - ☐ c. interesting.

2. The wolf was able to see Bertha easily because
   - ☐ a. she was so tall.
   - ☐ b. she was standing close to him.
   - ☐ c. her clothing was so clean and white.

3. There were no sheep in the Prince's park because
   - ☐ a. he didn't like animals.
   - ☐ b. there wasn't enough grass in the park.
   - ☐ c. his mother dreamed he might be killed by a sheep.

4. The young man's story succeeded in
   - ☐ a. winning applause from the aunt.
   - ☐ b. keeping the children interested and quiet for ten minutes.
   - ☐ c. bothering the other passengers.

HANDLE NEW VOCABULARY WORDS. The following questions check your vocabulary skills. Put an *x* in the box next to each correct answer.

1. The young man paused to let the picture he was describing sink into the children's imagination; then he resumed the story. The word *resumed* means
   - ☐ a. continued.
   - ☐ b. shouted.
   - ☐ c. disliked.

2. The children were not eager to hear the aunt's story, so they moved toward her slowly and listlessly. Define the word *listlessly.*
   - ☐ a. joyfully
   - ☐ b. quickly
   - ☐ c. without interest

3. The young man was annoyed at the girl because she kept repeating the same line of poetry in a firm and very audible voice. Which of the following phrases best defines the word *audible*?
   - ☐ a. unable to be heard
   - ☐ b. able to be heard
   - ☐ c. able to be seen

4. The aunt managed to hold back and suppress a gasp. What is the meaning of the word *suppress*?
   - ☐ a. stop or keep in
   - ☐ b. think about or consider
   - ☐ c. laugh at or chuckle

☐ × 5 = ☐

NUMBER CORRECT   YOUR SCORE

☐ × 5 = ☐

NUMBER CORRECT   YOUR SCORE

89

IDENTIFY STORY ELEMENTS. The following questions check your knowledge of story elements. Put an *x* in the box next to each correct answer.

1. What is the *setting* of the story?
   ☐ a. an automobile
   ☐ b. a railroad car
   ☐ c. an airplane

2. The *mood* of "The Story-Teller" is
   ☐ a. light and amusing.
   ☐ b. solemn and serious.
   ☐ c. very suspenseful.

3. What was the author's main *purpose* in writing the story?
   ☐ a. to teach or instruct the reader
   ☐ b. to convince or persuade the reader
   ☐ c. to amuse or entertain the reader

4. In "The Story-Teller," there is *conflict* between Bertha and the wolf and between
   ☐ a. the young man and the children.
   ☐ b. the young man and the aunt.
   ☐ c. the Prince and Bertha.

NOTE WORDS IN A PASSAGE. The following questions use the cloze technique to check your reading comprehension. Complete the paragraph by filling in each blank with one of the words listed below. Each word appears in the story. Since there are five words and four blanks, one of the words will not be used.

In 1830 a man _____1_____ Peter Cooper built a small locomotive that he called the *Tom Thumb*. Cooper maintained that his "iron horse" could run more _____2_____ than any real horse. A race was eventually held near Baltimore, Maryland. The "iron horse" took an early lead and seemed certain to _____3_____ . But with victory in sight, the "iron horse" slipped a belt, and the horse _____4_____ past it to win the race.

triumph   dashed

swiftly

appreciate   named

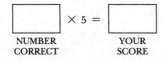

NUMBER CORRECT   × 5 =   YOUR SCORE

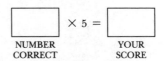

NUMBER CORRECT   × 5 =   YOUR SCORE

90

KNOW HOW TO READ CRITICALLY. The following questions check your critical thinking skills. Put an *x* in the box next to each correct answer.

1. It is likely that Bertha would have escaped from the wolf if
   ☐ a. she had attempted to run away.
   ☐ b. her medals for goodness had not clinked together.
   ☐ c. the scent of the bushes had been much stronger.

2. Which statement is true?
   ☐ a. After she heard his story, the aunt was annoyed with the story-teller.
   ☐ b. After she heard his story, the aunt praised the story-teller.
   ☐ c. The Prince allowed Bertha into the park because she loved flowers so much.

3. The children probably liked the young man's story so much because it
   ☐ a. was so similar to their aunt's stories.
   ☐ b. began in such an interesting way.
   ☐ c. provided an example of goodness that was punished, not rewarded.

4. In "The Story-Teller," the author, Saki, appears to be
   ☐ a. criticizing the young man.
   ☐ b. finding fault with the actions of the children.
   ☐ c. poking a bit of fun at the aunt.

Thinking for Writing and Discussion

- The young man had a lively imagination as well as the ability to think very quickly. Provide several examples to support that statement.
- Why did the aunt fear that the young man had very nearly ruined years of careful teaching? Was the aunt's concern realistic? Why or why not?
- Suppose the aunt had told the children about Bertha and the wolf. Think about how *she* might have concluded the tale. Give the aunt's ending to the story.

Use the boxes below to total your scores for the exercises.

☐ **T**ELL ABOUT THE STORY
+
☐ **H**ANDLE NEW VOCABULARY WORDS
+
☐ **I**DENTIFY STORY ELEMENTS
+
☐ **N**OTE WORDS IN A PASSAGE
+
☐ **K**NOW HOW TO READ CRITICALLY
▼
☐ **Total Score:** Story 8

☐ × 5 = ☐
NUMBER   YOUR
CORRECT   SCORE

9. Martinez' Treasure

by Manuela Williams Crosno

Meet the Author

Manuela Williams Crosno (1905–   ) enjoys writing about her beloved Southwest. A resident of New Mexico, she sets many of her stories in and around Santa Fe, Albuquerque, and Taos. In addition to writing short stories, Crosno is a gifted poet and a member of the New Mexico State Poetry Society. Her most recent collection is *The Other Side of Nowhere.* Crosno's poems and stories have appeared in *New Mexico Quarterly* and *New Mexico Magazine.*

There was once a man named Juan Martinez who lived near the mountains, but it was so long ago no one can remember just where he lived. He had a wife named Rosa, a burro whom he called Jose, and two goats. Rosa had a small flock of chickens. At one time Juan and Rosa had been young and carefree, but now they were quite old. A warm summer sun shining down many years had so wrinkled their faces that they seemed as old as the wrinkled hills about them.

They lived where the mountains meet the desert and the forest begins. Each day Martinez walked among the trees and gathered small pieces of wood. He loaded these on Jose's back, which had become scarred and bent from many loads. At one time Jose had moved slowly because he was lazy, as are all burros, but now the burden of age had been added to his indolence, so that he barely moved along in the midday heat.

For many years, Juan and Rosa had lived in a small house, which Juan proudly called their *casa*. From time to time they had repaired the house with adobe, which they patted on with their bare hands, until now all its sides bulged like buttresses. The roof leaned badly, as if it were trying to shelter its owners for their few remaining years and found the task almost too great.

Juan and Rosa were very poor. In summer, they raised beans and corn to eat through the winter, and chili peppers to season the beans. The red strings of peppers hanging over the roof of their *casa* in the fall were the only colorful thing about it. With the small amount of money Juan received for the firewood he sold, they were able to buy a bit of food—flour for the tortillas and, occasionally, cheese for the enchiladas. Their few items of clothing consisted of worn-out pieces their relatives no longer would wear.

Juan and Rosa had no children. Except when they went to the village, they seldom saw a living thing—just Jose, who was not good company, their two goats, the chickens, and a few lizards that darted from their path as they went about their work.

When they were young, they had made great plans for themselves. But trying to produce food from the dry soil had been difficult. Gradually they lost themselves in work and forgot how to laugh or play. Finally, they talked of nothing except their work and completely abandoned their early dreams. They forgot they had ever been happy, and they accepted their monotonous and meager living as a way of life. All they knew was work and more work.

The two people were busy all day long. Martinez would be gone for hours, loading old Jose's back with wood. The next day,

Martinez would go to the village, several miles away, to sell the wood. Then he would gather another load of wood, and so on, day in and day out.

For poor Rosa, each day was the same. She would rise early and milk the two goats. Then, unless there were many rains, she would drive the goats out to eat the grass that grew meagerly on the desert. She worked hard in the fields, with the goats close by.

Sometimes she baked in the oven, which was like those built by Indians who lived in the pueblos along the river. The round adobe oven looked like a huge beehive sitting on the ground. Rosa heated the oven by burning wood in it. When Rosa made tortillas, she ground the corn, and then flattened and shaped the cakes with her hands. The cakes came out white, with some brown spots. Juan always told Rosa they were the best tortillas he had ever tasted.

One evening Juan came home much later than usual. It had been dark for several hours. Rosa had stood at the window holding a candle, peering anxiously out into the darkness, looking for a sign of him. When he finally stood in the doorway, she noticed that his clothing was dusty and caked with mud. Jose stood behind him. Instead of the usual load of wood, a box or chest, about eighteen inches deep and wide and two feet long, was tied across the burro's sagging back. Together Juan and Rosa removed the box and dragged it inside, for it was very heavy and covered with hard-packed soil.

Juan told Rosa an interesting story. While Juan was gathering wood, Jose had wandered to the edge of a small arroyo. The burro's weight caused some soil on the side of the arroyo to give way, and Jose slid to the bottom of the ditch, a distance of a few feet. Juan walked down into the arroyo to get the burro. He saw the box sticking out of the side of the arroyo, where the earth had crumbled. All day he dug about it with sticks, only to find it was too heavy for him to lift onto the burro's back. He dragged the chest along the top of the arroyo to a place where the ditch was deeper than Jose was tall, and there he lowered it onto the burro's back and brought it home.

Rosa's first concern was for Juan. She gave him dry clothing and a bowl of hot chili. Then they could no longer contain their excitement, and they turned their attention to the box, wondering what it contained. But they could find no place where it might be opened; it had no lock, and its top could not be pried off. The chest was rusty, so they scraped it with knives and even washed its sides in an effort to find a way to open it. They worked very late by the light of the crude candle that Rosa had carefully made. Still, they found no way to open the box, and so they decided to sleep and try again in the morning.

At daybreak, they again tried to open the box. Remembering stories of hidden gold, they were certain the chest was filled with old Spanish coins. Therefore, they did not want anyone to know of their discovery. They had to find a way to open it themselves.

But promises of riches could not keep them from their work. Soon after the first warm glow of sunlight came through their window, habit called them to their usual tasks. They hid the box away under some old blankets and baskets and, all day, they thought about it and the treasure it contained.

Again they worked late into the night, trying to open the box. They could see small letters carved into the metal-like material, but neither of them had had the opportunity to learn to read. Above the letters was a single ornament, standing out from the chest as if for emphasis as well as design.

Juan and Rosa were strangely content now that they thought they were rich. They spent many hours trying to open the chest, and while they were working, a great change came over them. They became happy, and they remained so! Now that they had gold, they did not mind that they appeared poor. They knew they could buy fine clothing! They did not mind that Jose was old. They could buy many burros with the gold in the chest! They worked uncomplainingly, and they ate their meager food as if it, too, contained great richness.

Finally Martinez said to his wife, "We must tell no one about the box and we must think hard how to open it. Some day I will find how to open it!"

"That is right," she agreed. "We must tell no one!"

"Even if we could open the box," added her husband, "we would be afraid to keep the gold about. We would want to store it someplace. Here it is safely hidden—and we will leave it here as if we had stored it away! We are rich people!"

They put the chest away, hiding it carefully, and walked in lively steps around the room— almost dancing.

"Look, my Juan," said Rosa, "we are not so old!"

Now they felt as they had when they were young, so they began to do many things that were new to them. They did not work so long each day, and yet they seemed to get as much done as before. Juan sang half-remembered phrases of old songs in a shaky treble as he gathered wood. Rosa planted morning glories all around the *casa*, covering its barrenness.

Their blossoms were large and blue and made the old, brown adobe look beautiful! Juan and Rosa kept the goat corral and the chicken pen clean. They even tolerated Jose and brushed his tattered coat until it was almost shiny.

Happiness, it seemed, came to them in great amounts. Their relatives in the village noticed this change. There was a new freshness in Rosa's old, wrinkled cheeks, and Juan smiled so often that he seemed younger. Their eyes sparkled with gladness.

"Juan and Rosa are not so poor, after all," said their relatives, and, having more respect for them, they gave them better clothes to wear. One of Juan's brothers, Pancho, gave them a young burro to replace Jose. Pancho's wife scolded him for it later, but it brought much happiness to Juan. With the new burro, he could gather wood faster than ever and hurry back to his *casa* and the box containing his treasure. Jose was left to wander about on the desert and spend his time in idleness. Finally, he was given to Rosa's nephew's son, Cruz, a gentle lad who was kind to him.

So the days passed and Juan and Rosa knew great joy. They had not learned yet how to open the chest, but they thought that some day they would. It seemed not to matter greatly how soon.

The years quickly came and quickly went, and finally *los viejos*[1] died—first Rosa, and then Juan, who died at the home of his brother, Pancho.

After Juan's funeral, Pancho's wife said to her husband, "Go and get the burro you gave to Juan. He no longer needs it, and the beast will but die!"

So Pancho took his older brother Tomas

with him, and together they went to Juan's house to get the burro. They found the little mouse-colored animal standing dejectedly near the corral where Juan had left him several days earlier. But before they took him with them, they entered Juan's house and found the chest. The two brothers tried in vain to open it.

"This," they agreed, "is why Juan and Rosa did not seem poor! The box is so heavy, it must be filled with gold!"

Together they loaded the chest onto the wagon, hid it in Pancho's house under cover of darkness, and told no one, except Pancho's wife, of their discovery. They reasoned at once that they had done more to help Juan and Rosa than had their other brothers or sisters, so the chest was rightly theirs. They knew happiness as they dreamed of what they would do with the gold, because, like Juan and Rosa, they never doubted that they would find the chest filled with gold pieces. Pancho's wife made plans to be the richest, the most beautiful, and the finest clothed woman in the village. She spoke of money in such hushed tones that the villagers thought her husband was going to receive an inheritance.

Even though the brothers finally attacked the chest with heavy tools, as Juan and Rosa never would have done, they could not split it apart! Finally they grew impatient, and began to look for ways to get it open. Late one afternoon, Pancho stopped at the home of the village doctor, a learned man who could read well.

"Doctor Gardea," he said, "my wife has been complaining of a bad headache. I wish you would come to my *casa*." (This was not true, but Pancho's wife had agreed to pretend illness.)

It had already grown dark when Dr. Gardea came to Pancho's house. After talking with

---

1. **los viejos:** Spanish for "the old people."

the wife, he prescribed two days of absolute quiet. He had lived in the village long enough to know that she was considered a gossip and troublemaker, so he told himself, whimsically, that this would stop her talking for a few days. The doctor was a busy man and the woman's whisperings of wealth had not yet reached his ears.

He was about to take his leave when Pancho asked, "Have you ever seen this old chest? It has been in my family for years!" (Pancho was not one to be concerned with truth.) "It belonged to the father of my father, and to his father before him. It has been kept in the *casa* of Juan, my brother, and both Tomas and I have forgotten how to open it. Will you read for us what the letters say?"

The doctor stepped over to the chest and knelt beside it. Tomas and Pancho and Pancho's wife stood beside him trying to hide their excitement; their hearts pounded rapidly!

Silently, the doctor read the Latin words on the chest. Then he asked, "Are you sure you want to open the chest? You do remember the message?"

"Oh, yes!" replied the brothers together, "we want to open it!"

The doctor seemed reluctant. "In addition to the message, the letters tell how to open it," he remarked. With a quick pull, he tore aside one corner of the ornament. Then he unfastened the clasp that would allow the top to open. However, he did not lift the lid, but left the house.

Pancho closed the door and locked it carefully after the doctor had gone. Now the three people could not hide their excitement! Soon they would be rich! Already they could feel the gold pieces sliding through their fingers! They quickly opened the lid.

The firelight fell on the chest, which was filled with *santos*—wooden images of the saints! Hastily, in their anxiety to get at the treasure they thought was hidden away beneath the figures, they threw these out on the floor. They bruised and tore their hands. Soon the box was completely empty. There had been no worldly treasure in the chest.

The brothers argued with one another, and Pancho's wife became miserable. Now her neighbors would learn that Pancho was not to receive any wealth, that they were to remain poor, after all.

A thought came to her which she told to Pancho. "Perhaps Juan and Rosa took the gold and buried it near the house."

So Pancho and Tomas set about digging for the gold. They convinced themselves it had been removed from the chest and had been buried by Juan and Rosa. They dug up all the earth in and about the old *casa*, never finding any treasure. They spent several unhappy years digging, neglecting their crops, and growing poorer and more miserable. Finally, the brothers quarreled and went their separate ways.

Sometime later, Pancho met Dr. Gardea in the village. Perhaps the message on the chest told where the treasure was hidden!

Pancho demanded, "You will tell me what was carved into the old chest!"

The doctor believed firmly in the power of the written word. He hesitated. Then he repeated the curious message to Pancho. "Whoever owns this chest will be happy— so long as he opens it not!"

TELL ABOUT THE STORY. The following questions help you check your reading comprehension. Put an *x* in the box next to each correct answer.

1. Juan and Rosa believed that the old chest contained
   - ☐ a. gold coins.
   - ☐ b. wooden images.
   - ☐ c. heavy rocks.

2. Once they owned the wooden chest, Juan and Rosa
   - ☐ a. boasted to their neighbors about it.
   - ☐ b. bought many expensive items.
   - ☐ c. felt strangely content and much younger.

3. Pancho told Dr. Gardea that his wife
   - ☐ a. had a sore throat.
   - ☐ b. had a bad headache.
   - ☐ c. dreamed of becoming rich.

4. Pancho and Tomas dug up the earth around the old house because they
   - ☐ a. planned to plant crops there.
   - ☐ b. enjoyed the exercise.
   - ☐ c. were searching for buried gold.

HANDLE NEW VOCABULARY WORDS. The following questions check your vocabulary skills. Put an *x* in the box next to each correct answer.

1. After Juan died, the burro stood dejectedly near the corral where Juan had left him several days earlier. What is the meaning of the word *dejectedly*?
   - ☐ a. sadly
   - ☐ b. joyfully
   - ☐ c. guiltily

2. Dr. Gardea prescribed two days of quiet for Pancho's wife. Define the word *prescribed*.
   - ☐ a. received
   - ☐ b. questioned
   - ☐ c. ordered

3. At first, their monotonous life consisted of nothing but work and more work. The word *monotonous* means
   - ☐ a. very interesting.
   - ☐ b. lacking variety.
   - ☐ c. unusually dangerous.

4. Jose moved slowly because he was lazy, but the burden of age added to his indolence. What does *indolence* mean?
   - ☐ a. foolishness
   - ☐ b. happiness
   - ☐ c. laziness

☐ × 5 = ☐
NUMBER CORRECT   YOUR SCORE

☐ × 5 = ☐
NUMBER CORRECT   YOUR SCORE

IDENTIFY STORY ELEMENTS. The following questions check your knowledge of story elements. Put an *x* in the box next to each correct answer.

1. What happened first in the *plot* of the story?
   - ☐ a. Pancho ordered Dr. Gardea to read the message on the chest.
   - ☐ b. Tomas and Pancho went to Juan's house to get the burro.
   - ☐ c. Juan brought the wooden chest home.

2. Select the expression that best *characterizes* Pancho's wife.
   - ☐ a. generous and giving
   - ☐ b. quiet but friendly
   - ☐ c. greedy for wealth

3. The *mood* of "Martinez' Treasure" is
   - ☐ a. humorous.
   - ☐ b. serious.
   - ☐ c. terrifying.

4. Which of the following sentences illustrates a *conflict* involving a difference of ideas?
   - ☐ a. The brothers spent several years looking for the gold, but they never found any.
   - ☐ b. Rosa was curious about what the chest contained, but first she gave Juan some food.
   - ☐ c. Dr. Gardea didn't think the brothers should open the chest, but they disagreed and insisted.

	× 5 =	
NUMBER CORRECT		YOUR SCORE

NOTE WORDS IN A PASSAGE. The following questions use the cloze technique to check your reading comprehension. Complete the paragraph by filling in each blank with one of the words listed below. Each word appears in the story. Since there are five words and four blanks, one of the words will not be used.

In the southwestern part of the United States, many homes are constructed of a _____ called adobe. Adobe is
 ₁
the _____ name for sun-dried
 ₂
bricks. The clay from which these bricks are made is also called adobe. Adobe homes are popular in warm, dry _____
 ₃
climates. That is because adobe keeps a building cool by providing a natural _____ from the heat.
 ₄

impatient   material

Spanish

desert   shelter

	× 5 =	
NUMBER CORRECT		YOUR SCORE

99

KNOW HOW TO READ CRITICALLY. The following questions check your critical thinking skills. Put an *x* in the box next to each correct answer.

1. Dr. Gardea probably did not lift the lid of the chest because he
   - ☐ a. was not strong enough to move it.
   - ☐ b. already knew what was inside the chest.
   - ☐ c. respected the words of warning on the chest.

2. Juan and Rosa benefited from the old chest because it gave them
   - ☐ a. special rights and privileges.
   - ☐ b. the feeling that they were secure.
   - ☐ c. a fortune in gold.

3. Which statement is true?
   - ☐ a. Rosa eventually felt sorry that Juan had ever found the wooden chest.
   - ☐ b. The chest brought nothing but grief to Pancho and his wife.
   - ☐ c. Dr. Gardea refused to read Pancho the message on the chest.

4. It is fair to say that after Juan found the old chest, he and Rosa became rich because
   - ☐ a. happiness filled their lives.
   - ☐ b. they could purchase anything they wanted.
   - ☐ c. they took many wonderful vacations.

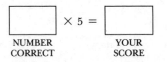

NUMBER
CORRECT

× 5 =

YOUR
SCORE

Thinking for Writing and Discussion

- Suppose the chest had actually contained gold. How do you think the gold would have changed Juan and Rosa's life? The lives of Pancho and his wife?
- Should Dr. Gardea have unfastened the clasp on the chest? Should he have revealed to Pancho the message on the chest? Support your opinions.
- The message carved into the chest stated, "Whoever owns this chest will be happy—so long as he opens it not." Show that those words proved fitting and true.

Use the boxes below to total your scores for the exercises.

☐ **T**ELL ABOUT THE STORY

+

☐ **H**ANDLE NEW VOCABULARY WORDS

+

☐ **I**DENTIFY STORY ELEMENTS

+

☐ **N**OTE WORDS IN A PASSAGE

+

☐ **K**NOW HOW TO READ CRITICALLY

▼

☐ **Total Score:** Story 9

100

10. The Ransom of Red Chief

by O. Henry

Meet the Author

O. Henry (1862–1910) is the pen name of William Sidney Porter, an author famous for short stories featuring his trademark surprise ending. Although O. Henry was born in North Carolina, he spent many years in New York City, a place that fascinated and delighted him. It provided the setting for many of his 273 short stories. Some of O. Henry's finest stories are collected in *The Four Million* and *The Voice of the City*.

*I*t looked like a good thing: but wait till I tell you. We were down south, in Alabama—Bill Driscoll and myself—when this kidnapping idea struck us. It was, as Bill expressed it afterward, "during a moment of mental madness." But we didn't find that out till later.

There was a town down there, as flat as a pancake, and called Summit, of course. It contained as harmless and self-satisfied a class of citizens as ever clustered around a Maypole.

Bill and me had a joint capital of about six hundred dollars, and we needed just two thousand dollars more to pull off a phony real estate scheme in western Illinois. We talked it over on the front steps of the hotel.

"Love of children by their parents," says I, "is especially strong in rural communities like Summit. Therefore, and for other good reasons, a kidnapping project here ought to go well."

We knew that unlike big cities that send out detectives and reporters on such things, Summit couldn't come after us with anything stronger than a sheriff and some deputies, and maybe some lazy and lackadaisical bloodhounds and an angry editorial or two in the local *Weekly Farmers' Journal.* So it looked good.

We selected for our victim the only child of a prominent citizen named Ebenezer Dorset. The father was a respectable and virtuous banker. The kid was a boy of ten with bright red hair and freckles. Bill and me figured that Ebenezer would melt down for a ransom of two thousand dollars to the cent. But wait till I tell you.

About two miles from Summit was a little mountain covered with dense bushes. On the rear elevation of this mountain was a cave. There we stored our provisions.

One evening after sundown, we drove past old Dorset's house. The kid was in the street, throwing rocks at a kitten on the opposite fence.

"Hey, little boy!" says Bill, "would you like to have a bag of candy and a nice ride?"

The boy catches Bill neatly in the eye with a piece of brick.

"That will cost the old man an extra five hundred dollars," says Bill, climbing out of the car.

That boy put up a fight like a welterweight champion bear. But at last we got him into the car and drove away. We took him up to the cave, and after dark I drove the car to the little village three miles away, where we had hired it, and then I walked back to the mountain.

Bill was pasting a batch of bandages over the scratches and bruises on his features. There was a fire burning behind the big rock at the entrance of the cave, and the boy was watching a pot of boiling coffee, with two buzzard tail feathers stuck in his red hair. He points a stick at me when I come up, and says:

"Ha! Do you dare to enter the camp of Red Chief, the terror of the plains?"

"He's all right now," says Bill, rolling up his trousers and examining some bruises on his shins. "We've been playing some games. I'm Old Hank, the Trapper. That kid can kick hard!"

Yes, sir, that boy seemed to be having the time of his life. The fun of camping out in a cave had made him forget that he was a captive himself. He smiled and immediately gave me the name Snake-eye, the Spy.

Then we had supper, and he filled his mouth full of bacon and bread and gravy, and began to talk. He made a during-dinner speech something like this:

"I like this fine. I never camped out before, but I had a pet 'possum once, and I was nine last birthday. I hate to go to school. Rats ate up sixteen of Jimmy Talbot's aunt's speckled hen's eggs. I want some more gravy. Does the trees moving make the wind blow? We had five puppies. What makes your nose so red, Hank? My father has lots of money. Are the stars hot? I whipped Ed Walker twice, Saturday. I don't like girls. You don't dare catch toads unless with a string. Do oxen make any noise? Why are oranges round? Have you got beds to sleep on in this cave? Amos Murray has got six toes. A parrot can talk, but a monkey or a fish can't. How many does it take to make twelve?"

Every now and then he would pick up his stick rifle and point it at Old Hank. That boy had Bill terrorized from the start.

"Red Chief," says I to the kid, "would you like to go home?"

"Aw, what for?" says he. "I don't have any fun at home. I hate to go to school. I like to camp out. You won't take me back home again, Snake-eye, will you?"

"Not right away," says I. "We'll stay here in the cave a while."

"All right!" says he. "That'll be fine. I never had such fun in all my life."

We went to bed about eleven o'clock. We spread down some wide blankets and quilts and put Red Chief between us. We weren't afraid he'd run away. He kept us awake for three hours, jumping up and reaching for his rifle and screeching: "Hist! pard," in mine and Bill's ears, as the fancied crackle of a twig or the rustle of a leaf revealed to his young imagination the stealthy approach of an outlaw band. At last, I fell into a troubled sleep, and dreamed that I had been kidnapped and chained to a tree by a ferocious pirate with red hair.

Just at daybreak, I was awakened by a series of awful screams from Bill. They weren't yells, or howls, or shouts, or whoops, or yawps, such as you'd expect—they were simply terrifying screams. It's an awful thing to hear a strong, desperate, fat man screaming wildly in a camp at daybreak.

I jumped up to see what the matter was. Red Chief was having some fun. He was sitting on Bill's chest, and in one hand he was waving around the long, sharp knife we used for slicing bacon.

I got the knife away from the kid and made him lie down again. But from that moment, Bill's spirit was broken. He lay down on the side of his bed, but he never closed an eye in sleep again as long as that boy was with us. I dozed off for a while, but along toward sunup I sat up and leaned against a rock.

"What are you getting up so soon for, Sam?" asked Bill.

"Me?" says I. "Oh, I got kind of a pain in my shoulder. I thought sitting up would rest it."

"You're a liar!" says Bill. "The kid's made you jumpy, too. Ain't it awful, Sam? Do you think anybody will pay out money to get a little imp like that back home?"

"Sure," said I. "A rowdy kid like that is just the kind that parents dote on. Now you and the Chief get up and cook breakfast, while I go up on the top of this mountain and look around."

I went up on the peak of the little mountain and ran my eye over the whole area. Over toward Summit I expected to see the good villagers, armed with scythes and pitchforks, beating the countryside looking for the wicked kidnappers. But what I saw was a peaceful landscape with one man plowing some ground with an old mule. Nobody was dragging the creek. No messengers dashed back and forth bringing word that there was no news to the worried parents. A calm, sleepy, peaceful atmosphere hung over everything.

"Perhaps," says I to myself, "it has not yet been discovered that the kid is missing," and I went down the mountain to breakfast.

When I got to the cave I found Bill backed up against the side of it, breathing hard, and the boy threatening to smash him with a rock as big as a coconut.

"He put a red-hot boiled potato down my back," explained Bill, "and then mashed it with his foot, and I boxed his ears. Have you got a gun about you, Sam?"

I took the rock away from the boy and kind of patched up the argument. "I'll fix you," says the kid to Bill. "No man ever yet struck Red Chief and got away with it. You better beware!"

After breakfast the kid takes a piece of leather with strings wrapped around it out of his pocket and goes outside the cave unwinding it.

"What's he up to now?" says Bill, anxiously. "You don't think he'll run away, do you, Sam?"

"No fear of it," says I. "He don't seem to be much of a homebody. But we've got to fix up some plan about the ransom. There don't seem to be much excitement around Summit on account of his disappearance, but maybe they haven't realized yet that he's gone. His folks may think he's spending the night with Aunt Jane or one of the neighbors. Anyhow, he'll be missed today. Tonight we must get a message to his father demanding the two thousand dollars for his return."

Just then we heard a kind of war whoop, such as David might have emitted when he knocked out the champion Goliath. It was a sling that Red Chief had pulled out of his pocket, and he was whirling it around his head.

I ducked, and heard a heavy thud and a kind of a sigh from Bill, like a horse lets out when you take his saddle off. A rock the size of an egg had caught Bill just behind his left ear. His legs gave way and he fell in the fire across the frying pan of hot water for washing the dishes. I dragged him out and poured cold water on his head for half an hour.

By and by, Bill sits up and feels behind his ear and starts babbling.

"Take it easy," says I. "You'll come to your senses presently."

Bill looks at me and says, "You won't go away and leave me here alone, will you, Sam?"

I went out and caught that boy and shook him until his freckles rattled.

"If you don't behave," says I, "I'll take you straight home. Now, are you going to be good, or not?"

"I was only kidding around," says he sullenly. "I didn't mean to hurt Old Hank. But what did he hit me for? I'll behave, Snake-eye, if you won't send me home, and if you'll let me play Scout today."

"I don't know the game," says I. "That's for you and Mr. Bill to decide. He'll play with you today. I'm going away for a while on business. Now you come in and make friends with him and say you are sorry for hurting him, or home you go, at once."

I made him and Bill shake hands, and then I took Bill aside and told him I was going to Poplar Cove, a little village three miles from the cave, to find out what I could about how the kidnapping had been regarded in Summit. Also, I thought it best to send a strict letter to old man Dorset that day, demanding the ransom and dictating how it should be paid.

"You know, Sam," says Bill, "I've stood by you without batting an eye in earthquakes, fire, and flood—in police raids, train robberies, and cyclones. I never lost my nerve yet till we kidnapped that two-legged skyrocket of a kid. He's got me going. You won't leave me long with him, will you, Sam?"

"I'll be back sometime this afternoon," says I. "You must keep the boy amused and quiet till I return. And now we'll write the letter to old Dorset."

Bill and I got paper and pencil and worked on the letter while Red Chief strutted up and down, guarding the mouth of the cave. Bill begged me tearfully to make the ransom fifteen hundred dollars instead of two thousand. "I ain't attempting," says he, "to make light of parental affection, but we're dealing with humans, and it ain't human for anybody to give up two thousand dollars for that forty-pound chunk of freckled wildcat. I'm willing to take a chance at fifteen hundred dollars. You can charge the difference to me."

For Bill's sake, I agreed, and we wrote a letter that ran this way:

Ebenezer Dorset:

We have your boy concealed in a place far from Summit. It is useless for you or the most skillful detectives to attempt to find him. Absolutely, the only terms on which you can have him restored to you are these: We demand fifteen hundred dollars in large bills for his return. The money is to be left at midnight tonight at the same spot and in the same box as your reply.

If you agree to these terms, send your answer in writing by a solitary messenger tonight at half-past eight o'clock. After crossing Owl Creek, on the road to Poplar Cove, there are three large trees about a hundred yards apart, close to the fence of the wheat field on the right-hand side. At the bottom of the fence post, opposite the third tree, will be found a small cardboard box.

The messenger will place the answer in this box and return immediately to Summit.

If you attempt any treachery or fail to meet our demand as stated, you will never see your boy again.

If you pay the money as demanded, he will be returned to you safe and well within three hours. These terms are final, and if you do not agree to them no further communication will be attempted.

Two Desperate Men

I addressed this letter to Dorset, and put it in my pocket. As I was about to start, the kid comes up to me and says:

"Aw, Snake-eye, you said I could play Scout while you was gone."

"Play it, of course," says I. "Mr. Bill will play with you. What kind of a game is it?"

"I'm Scout," says Red Chief, "and I have to ride to the stockade."

"All right," says I. "It sounds harmless to me. I guess Mr. Bill will help you play the game."

"What am I to do?" asks Bill, looking at the kid suspiciously.

"You are the hoss," says Scout. "Get down on your hands and knees. How can I ride to the stockade without a hoss?"

"You'd better keep him interested," said I, "till we get the scheme going. Loosen up."

Bill gets down on his all fours, and a look comes in his eye like a rabbit's when you catch it in a trap.

"How far is it to the stockade, kid?" he asks, in a husky manner of voice.

"Ninety miles," says Scout. "And you have to really move to get there on time. Whoa, now!" Scout jumps on Bill's back and digs his heels in his side.

"For heaven's sake," says Bill, "hurry back, Sam, as soon as you can. I wish we hadn't made the ransom more than a thousand. Say, you quit kicking me or I'll get up and warm you good."

I walked over to Poplar Cove and sat around the post office and store, talking with the locals that came in to trade. Finally, someone says that he hears Summit is all upset on account of Ebenezer Dorset's boy having been lost or stolen. That was all I wanted to know. I bought some coffee beans, referred casually to the price of black-eyed peas, mailed my letter, and left. The postmaster said the mail carrier would come by in an hour to take the mail on to Summit.

When I got back to the cave, Bill and the boy were not to be found. I explored the vicinity of the cave and gave a couple of shouts, but there was no answer.

So I sat down on a mossy bank to await developments.

In about half an hour I heard the bushes rustle, and Bill stumbles out into the little glade in front of the cave. Behind him was the kid, stepping very softly, with a big grin on his face. Bill stopped, took off his hat, and wiped his face with a red handkerchief. The kid stopped about eight feet behind him.

"Sam," says Bill, "I suppose you'll think I'm a traitor, but I couldn't help it. I'm a grown person who can take care of himself, but there is a time when all systems of self-defense fail. The boy is gone. I have sent him home. All is off. I tried to be faithful to our plan, but there came a limit."

"What's the trouble, Bill?" I asks him.

"I was rode," says Bill, "the ninety miles to the stockade, not barring an inch. Then I was given oats. Sand ain't a tasty substitute. And then, for an hour I had to try to explain to him why there was nothin' in holes, how a road can run both ways, and what makes the grass green. I tell you, Sam, a human can only stand so much. I takes him by the neck of his clothes and drags him down the mountain. On the way he kicks my legs black and blue from the knees down, and I've got to have two or three bites on my thumb and hand treated.

"But he's gone"—continues Bill—"gone home. I showed him the road to Summit and kicked him about eight feet nearer there at one kick. I'm sorry we lose the ransom, but it was either that or Bill Driscoll to the madhouse."

Bill is huffing and puffing, but there is a look of indescribable peace and content on his face.

"Bill," says I, "there isn't any heart disease in your family, is there?"

"No," says Bill, "nothing. Why?"

"Then you might turn around," says I, "and have a look behind you."

Bill turns and sees the boy, and goes pale, and sits down on the grass and begins to pick aimlessly at little sticks. For an hour I was afraid for his mind. And then I told him that my idea was to put the whole plan through immediately and that we would get the ransom and be off with it by midnight if old Dorset went along with our proposition. So Bill braced up enough to give the kid a weak sort of a smile and a promise to play war with him as soon as he felt a little better.

I had a scheme for picking up that ransom without danger of being caught that was so good it could be used by professional kid-nappers. The tree under which the answer was to be left—and the money later on—was close to the road fence with large, bare fields on all sides. If a sheriff and a gang of deputies should be watching for anyone to come for the note, they could see him a long way off crossing the fields or in the road. But no, sirree! Long before half-past eight I was up in that tree as well hidden as a tree toad, waiting for the messenger to arrive.

Exactly on time, a boy rides up the road on a bicycle, locates the cardboard box at the foot of the fence post, slips a folded piece of paper into it, and pedals away again back toward Summit.

I waited an hour and then concluded it was safe. I slid down the tree, got the note, made my way along the fence till I got to the woods, and was back at the cave in another half an hour. I opened the note, got near the lantern, and read it to Bill. It said this:

Two Desperate Men,

Gentlemen: I received your letter today in regard to the ransom you ask for the return of my son. I think you are a little high in your demands, and I hereby make you a counter-proposition, which I am inclined to believe you will accept. You bring Johnny home and pay me two hundred and fifty dollars in cash, and I agree to take him off your hands. You had better come at night, for the neighbors believe he is lost, and I couldn't be responsible for what they would do to anybody they saw bringing him back.

Very respectfully,
Ebenezer Dorset

"Great pirates of Penzance!" says I. "Of all the impudent—"

But I glanced at Bill, and hesitated. He had the most appealing look in his eyes I ever saw.

"Sam," says he, "what's two hundred and fifty dollars, after all? We've got the money. One more night of this kid will drive me out of my mind. I think Mr. Dorset's a real gentleman for making us such a generous offer. You ain't going to let the chance go, are you?"

"Tell you the truth, Bill," says I, "the kid has somewhat got on my nerves, too. We'll take him home, pay the ransom, and make our getaway."

We took him home that night. We got him to go by telling him that his father had bought a silver-handled rifle and a pair of moccasins for him, and we were going to hunt bears the next day.

It was just twelve o'clock when we knocked at Ebenezer's front door. Just at the moment when I should have been taking the fifteen hundred dollars from the box under the tree, according to the original plan, Bill was counting out two hundred and fifty dollars into Dorset's hand.

When the kid found out we were going to leave him at home, he started to howl and fastened himself as tight as a leech to Bill's leg. His father peeled him away gradually.

"How long can you hold him?" asks Bill.

"I'm not as strong as I used to be," says old Dorset, "but I think I can promise you ten minutes."

"Enough," says Bill. "In ten minutes I shall cross the Central, Southern, and Middle Western states, and be legging it trippingly for the Canadian border."

And, as dark as it was, and as fat as Bill was, and as good a runner as I am, he was a good mile and a half out of Summit before I could catch up with him.

TELL ABOUT THE STORY. The following questions help you check your reading comprehension. Put an *x* in the box next to each correct answer.

1. Bill and Sam thought that Summit was a good place for a kidnapping because
   - ☐ a. it didn't have detectives or a large police force.
   - ☐ b. most of the citizens in Summit were wealthy.
   - ☐ c. the people there didn't care about the law.

2. While he was at the camp on the mountain, Red Chief
   - ☐ a. was very frightened and pleaded to go home.
   - ☐ b. complained that he missed his friends at school.
   - ☐ c. seemed to be having the time of his life.

3. Bill begged Sam to
   - ☐ a. make the ransom fifteen hundred dollars instead of two thousand.
   - ☐ b. increase the ransom because the boy caused so much trouble.
   - ☐ c. give up his life of crime.

4. Ebenezer Dorset's letter suggested that the kidnappers
   - ☐ a. release Johnny and give him directions for getting home.
   - ☐ b. bring Johnny to the sheriff's office at once.
   - ☐ c. bring Johnny home after giving his father two hundred and fifty dollars in cash.

☐ × 5 = ☐
NUMBER
CORRECT   YOUR
              SCORE

HANDLE NEW VOCABULARY WORDS. The following questions check your vocabulary skills. Put an *x* in the box next to each correct answer.

1. Johnny's father was a prominent citizen, a respected banker. As used here, the word *prominent* means
   - ☐ a. very tall.
   - ☐ b. well known or important.
   - ☐ c. noisy or loud.

2. When he was struck by a rock from the slingshot, Bill emitted a loud shout. What does *emitted* mean?
   - ☐ a. threatened
   - ☐ b. argued
   - ☐ c. gave out

3. The kidnappers were not afraid of some lazy and lackadaisical bloodhounds. Which expression best defines the word *lackadaisical*?
   - ☐ a. fierce and ferocious
   - ☐ b. swift and powerful
   - ☐ c. not very interested

4. All during the night the boy kept jumping up as he listened carefully for the stealthy approach of an outlaw band. The word *stealthy* means
   - ☐ a. sly.
   - ☐ b. obvious.
   - ☐ c. vivid.

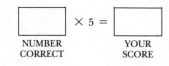

☐ × 5 = ☐
NUMBER
CORRECT   YOUR
              SCORE

IDENTIFY STORY ELEMENTS. The following questions check your knowledge of story elements. Put an *x* in the box next to each correct answer.

1. Who is the *narrator* of "The Ransom of Red Chief"?
   - ☐ a. Sam
   - ☐ b. Bill
   - ☐ c. Johnny

2. What was the author's *purpose* in writing the story?
   - ☐ a. to shock or frighten the reader
   - ☐ b. to amuse or entertain the reader
   - ☐ c. to teach the reader an important lesson

3. Judging by "The Ransom of Red Chief," what is true of O. Henry's *style* of writing?
   - ☐ a. His stories contain no dialogue.
   - ☐ b. His stories contain many long, descriptive poetic passages.
   - ☐ c. His stories conclude with a surprise.

4. The major *conflict* in the story is between
   - ☐ a. the citizens of Summit and the kidnappers.
   - ☐ b. Ebenezer Dorset and Sam.
   - ☐ c. Bill Driscoll and Red Chief.

NOTE WORDS IN A PASSAGE. The following questions use the cloze technique to check your reading comprehension. Complete the paragraph by filling in each blank with one of the words listed below. Each word appears in the story. Since there are five words and four blanks, one of the words will not be used.

Every year, many _____ in the
1
United States send letters and cards to their pen pals around the world. Sending and receiving mail is fun, and the _____ is sometimes educational. You can learn first-
2
hand about the customs and habits of families who live in _____ thousands of
3
miles away. And occasionally pen pals have a _____ to meet and see each other.
4

communication   chance

communities

children   casually

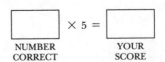

NUMBER   YOUR
CORRECT   SCORE

NUMBER   YOUR
CORRECT   SCORE

109

KNOW HOW TO READ CRITICALLY. The following questions check your critical thinking skills. Put an *x* in the box next to each correct answer.

1. The town was "as flat as a pancake, and called Summit. . . ." The humor here is based on the fact that
   □ a. pancakes are not flat.
   □ b. pancakes are never served in Summit.
   □ c. a summit is a *high* place.

2. Ebenezer Dorset's letter suggests that the neighbors were
   □ a. upset that Johnny had been kidnapped.
   □ b. delighted that Johnny had been kidnapped.
   □ c. organizing a search party to find Johnny.

3. The concluding paragraph of the story indicates that Bill
   □ a. couldn't wait to get away from Red Chief.
   □ b. had actually grown fond of the high-spirited boy.
   □ c. hoped to return to Summit before too long.

4. In "The Ransom of Red Chief," it is fair to say that
   □ a. Ebenezer Dorset was very worried about his son.
   □ b. Johnny was looking forward to going home.
   □ c. the kidnappers became the victims of their "victim."

	× 5 =	
NUMBER CORRECT		YOUR SCORE

Thinking for Writing and Discussion

● In addition to constructing humorous situations and characters, O. Henry was very skilled at writing humorous phrases and descriptions. For example, Sam says, "I went out and caught that boy and shook him until his freckles rattled." Look back through the story. Identify several phrases or descriptions that you found especially amusing.

● In his letter, Ebenezer Dorset told the kidnappers that he was making them a proposition that he was "inclined to believe" they would accept. Why was Mr. Dorset so certain they would agree to his offer?

● Suppose that the story concluded with a letter from Red Chief to Snake-eye and Old Hank. What do you think the letter would say?

Use the boxes below to total your scores for the exercises.

	TELL ABOUT THE STORY
+	
	HANDLE NEW VOCABULARY WORDS
+	
	IDENTIFY STORY ELEMENTS
+	
	NOTE WORDS IN A PASSAGE
+	
	KNOW HOW TO READ CRITICALLY
▼	
	Total Score: Story 10

11. The Bet

by Anton Chekhov

Meet the Author
Anton Chekhov (1860–1904) is considered one of Russia's greatest writers. The son of poor parents, he managed to enter the University of Moscow after graduating from high school. Later he became a medical doctor. Chekhov is famous for the vivid characters he created in his short stories and his humorous, touching dramas. His plays *The Cherry Orchard, The Three Sisters,* and *The Sea Gull* remain popular and are still performed frequently around the world.

*I*t was a dark autumn night. The old banker was pacing from corner to corner of his study, recalling to his mind the party he had given in the autumn fifteen years ago. There had been many clever people at the party and much interesting conversation. They talked, among other things, of capital punishment—the death penalty. The guests, for the most part, disapproved of it. Some of them thought that the death penalty should be replaced by life imprisonment.

"I don't agree with you," said the host to one of his guests. "In my opinion, the death penalty is more moral and kinder than life imprisonment. Execution kills instantly, whereas life imprisonment kills by degrees. Who is the more humane executioner—the one who kills you in a few seconds or the one who draws the life out of you slowly, over years?"

"They're both equally wrong," said another guest, "for both take away life."

Among the people present was a lawyer, a

111

young man of about twenty-five years of age. On being asked his opinion, he said, "The death penalty and life imprisonment seem to me equally cruel. But if I were offered a choice between them, I would certainly choose the second. It's better to live somehow than not to live at all."

There followed a lively discussion. The banker, who was then younger and more nervous, suddenly lost his temper. Banging his fist on the table, he turned to the young lawyer and cried out, "It's a lie. I bet you two million rubles you wouldn't be able to stay in a cell even for five years."

"If you mean it seriously," replied the lawyer, "then I'll bet. I'll stay not five years but fifteen."

"Fifteen! Done!" cried the banker. "I'll bet two million rubles."

"Agreed," said the lawyer. "You stake two million rubles; I stake my freedom."

So this wild, ridiculous bet came to pass. The banker, who at that time had too much money to count, was beside himself with rapture. During supper he said to the lawyer, jokingly, "Come to your senses, young man, before it's too late. Two million rubles mean nothing to me. But you stand to lose three or four of the best years of your life. I say three or four because you'll never stick it out any longer. The fact that you have *volunteered* to go to prison and were not *forced* to do so will make it much harder for you. The idea that you can free yourself whenever you want will poison your entire time in the cell and make it all the more miserable. I pity you."

And now, fifteen years later, the banker paced from corner to corner of his study, remembering all of this. He asked himself, "Why did I make that bet? What was the good of it? The lawyer loses fifteen years of his life, and I throw away two million rubles. Will it convince people that the death penalty is worse or better than imprisonment for life? No, not at all. On my part, it was the whim of a well-fed man. On the lawyer's part, it was greed for money."

He recollected further what had happened after the dinner party. It was decided that the lawyer would be locked up in a cottage in the banker's garden. It was agreed that during the time he was there, the lawyer would be watched very closely. He would be deprived of the right to leave the cottage, to see living people, to hear human voices, and to receive letters and newspapers. He was permitted to have a musical instrument, to read books, to write letters, to eat and to drink. According to the agreement, he could communicate with the outside world—but only in silence—through a little window specially constructed for this purpose. Everything he needed—books, music, paper, and so forth—he could receive by sending a note through the window.

The agreement set forth all the details, and it obliged the lawyer to remain exactly fifteen years—from twelve o'clock on November 14, 1870, to twelve o'clock on November 14, 1885. The slightest attempt to violate the conditions—to escape, if only for two minutes before the time—would free the banker from the obligation to pay the lawyer the two million rubles.

During the first year of imprisonment, the lawyer, as far as it was possible to judge from his short notes, suffered terribly from loneliness and boredom. From his cottage, day and night, came the sound of the piano. During that first year the lawyer asked for books of light reading: novels with a love interest, stories of crime and fantasy, comedies, and so forth.

In the second year the piano was heard no longer, and the lawyer asked for great books—the classics. In the fifth year, music was heard again. Those who watched him said that during the whole of that year he seemed to spend much time thinking. He yawned often and talked angrily to himself. Books he did not read. Sometimes at night he would sit down to write. He would write for a long time and tear it all up in the morning. More than once he was heard to weep.

In the second half of the sixth year, the prisoner began to study languages, philosophy, and history. He studied these subjects with such zeal that the banker hardly had time to get books enough for him. For a period of four years, about six hundred volumes were brought at his request. During this time, the banker received the following letter from the prisoner:

My dear jailer,

I am writing these lines to you in six different languages. Show them to experts and let them read them. If they cannot find a single mistake in any of the languages, please order a gun to be fired off in the garden. When I hear the noise, I shall know that my studying has not been in vain. The geniuses of all ages and countries speak in different languages. But in all of them the same flame burns. Oh, if you knew my heavenly happiness now that I can understand them!

The prisoner's wish was granted. At the banker's order, two shots were fired in the garden.

Later on, after the tenth year, the lawyer sat immovable in front of his table and read only the Bible. The banker found it strange that a man who in four years had mastered six hundred difficult volumes should spend nearly a year reading one book, which seemed easy to understand and was by no means thick.

During the last two years of his confinement, the prisoner read an extraordinary amount, quite haphazardly. Sometimes he would read books about science. Then he would read poetry or the plays of Shakespeare. He read as though he were swimming in the sea among broken pieces of wreckage, and in his desire to save his life was eagerly grasping one piece after another.

The banker recalled all of this and thought, "Tomorrow at twelve o'clock he will receive his freedom. Under the agreement, I shall have to pay him two million rubles. If I pay the money, it's all over with me. I'll be ruined forever."

Fifteen years before, the banker had too many millions to count, but now he was afraid to ask himself which he had more of, money or debts. He had gambled on the stock exchange, unable to stop himself from taking wild risks. These had gradually forced his business to decay. The once fearless, self-confident, proud man of business had now become an ordinary banker, one who trembled at every rise and fall in the market.

"That cursed bet," murmured the old man, clutching his head in despair. "The lawyer's only forty years old. He will take my last rubles, marry, enjoy life, and I will look on like an envious beggar and hear the same words from him every day: 'I'm obliged to you for the happiness of my life. Let *me* help you now.' No, it's too much! The only escape from

113

bankruptcy and disgrace—is that the man should die!"

The clock had just struck three. The banker was listening. In the house everyone was asleep, and one could hear only the wind whistling outside the windows. Trying to make no sound, the banker took from his safe the key to the cottage door, which had not been opened for fifteen years. He put on his overcoat and went out of the house. The garden was dark and bleak. It was raining. A damp, penetrating wind howled loudly. Though he strained his eyes, the banker could see neither the ground nor the trees. Approaching the cottage, he called the watchman twice. There was no answer. The watchman had evidently taken shelter from the bad weather and was now asleep somewhere in the kitchen or the greenhouse.

"If I have the courage to fulfill my intention," thought the old man, "the suspicion will fall on the watchman."

In the darkness he made his way toward the cottage and, trembling with agitation, peeped into the little window.

Inside, in the prisoner's room, a candle was burning dimly. The banker saw that the prisoner was sitting by the table. Only his back and his hands were visible. Open books were strewn on the table, on the two chairs, and on the carpet near the table.

Five minutes passed, and the prisoner never once stirred. Fifteen years of confinement had taught him to sit motionless. The banker tapped on the window with his finger, but the prisoner made no movement in reply. Then the banker put the key into the lock. The rusty lock gave a hoarse groan, and the door creaked. The banker expected instantly to hear a cry of surprise and the sound of steps. Three minutes passed, and the cottage was as quiet as it had been before. He made up his mind to enter.

In front of the table sat a man unlike an ordinary human being. He was like a skeleton, with tight-drawn skin, long hair, and a shaggy beard. The color of his face was yellow, his cheeks were sunken, and the hand upon which he leaned his hairy head was so lean and skinny that it was painful to look at. His hair was already silvering with gray, and no one who glanced at his hollow face would have believed that he was only forty years old. On the table near his bent head lay a sheet of paper on which something was written in tiny letters.

"Poor devil," thought the banker, "he's asleep and probably seeing millions of rubles in his dreams. I could easily throw this half-dead thing on the bed, smother him in a moment with the pillow, and the most careful examination would reveal no trace of unnatural death. But first let me read what he has written here."

The banker took the sheet of paper from the table and read:

Tomorrow at twelve o'clock I shall obtain my freedom and the right to mix with people again. But before I leave this room and see the sun, I think it necessary to say a few words to you. On my own clear conscience, I declare to you that I despise the things that you call the blessings of the world.

For fifteen years I have carefully studied earthly life. True, I saw neither the earth nor its people, but in your books I experienced all. In your books I climbed to the summits of the highest mountains and saw from there how the sun rose in the morning and how, in the evening, it painted the sky, the ocean, and the mountain ridges with purple gold. From the mountain I saw how the lightning glimmered above me, piercing the clouds. I saw green forests, fields, rivers, lakes, cities. In your books I cast myself into bottomless abysses, worked miracles, conquered whole countries.

Your books gave me wisdom. All human thought, down through the ages, I have taken into my brain.

And I despise those worldly goods that you worship above all. For you love and cherish riches rather than ideals. You are mad and have gone the wrong way. You take falsehood for truth and ugliness for beauty. I am amazed at you, who have bartered heaven for earth. I do not want to understand you.

That I may truly show you how little I think of the money you worship so much, I waive my right to the two million rubles which I once dreamed of as paradise, and which I now hold in contempt. To deprive myself of the right to the rubles, I shall come out from here *five minutes before* the agreed-upon time. Thus I shall violate the agreement and give up my right to the money.

When he had read these words, the banker put the sheet of paper on the table, kissed the head of the strange man, and began to weep. He went out of the cottage. Never at any other time had he felt such contempt for himself as now. Arriving home, he lay down on the bed, but upset and tearful, he had a difficult time falling asleep.

The next day, just before noon, the watchman came running to the banker and told him that he had seen the man who lived in the cottage climb through a window and jump down into the garden. The man had then run off and disappeared.

The banker at once went with his servants to the cottage and established the fact that the prisoner had left. To avoid unnecessary rumors, the banker took the note that the man had written and carefully locked it in his safe.

TELL ABOUT THE STORY. The following questions help you check your reading comprehension. Put an *x* in the box next to each correct answer.

1. The lawyer wagered that he could remain locked up alone for
   ☐ a. exactly five years.
   ☐ b. fifteen years.
   ☐ c. his entire life.

2. Over the course of time, the banker
   ☐ a. grew richer than ever.
   ☐ b. gave a great deal of money to charity.
   ☐ c. suffered many business losses.

3. While he was at the cottage, the prisoner spent most of his time
   ☐ a. reading and studying.
   ☐ b. writing short stories and novels.
   ☐ c. doing crossword puzzles and similar games.

4. In his letter to the banker, the prisoner stated that he planned to
   ☐ a. claim the two million rubles at once.
   ☐ b. travel around the world to see interesting places.
   ☐ c. give up his right to the money.

HANDLE NEW VOCABULARY WORDS. The following questions check your vocabulary skills. Put an *x* in the box next to each correct answer.

1. It was agreed that the lawyer would be deprived of the right to leave the cottage or to see living people. The word *deprived* means
   ☐ a. aided or assisted.
   ☐ b. questioned or asked.
   ☐ c. prevented or kept from having.

2. Trembling with agitation, the banker peeped into the little window. Which of the following phrases best defines the word *agitation*?
   ☐ a. a troubled state of mind
   ☐ b. a clear conscience
   ☐ c. a pleasant task

3. The slightest attempt to violate the agreement would cause the lawyer to lose the bet. As used in that sentence, what is the meaning of the word *violate*?
   ☐ a. offer
   ☐ b. break
   ☐ c. ponder

4. When the lawyer agreed to the terms of the bet, the banker was "beside himself with rapture." The word *rapture* means
   ☐ a. sorrow or sadness.
   ☐ b. great disappointment.
   ☐ c. a strong feeling of joy.

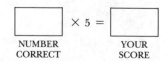

☐ × 5 = ☐

NUMBER   YOUR
CORRECT   SCORE

☐ × 5 = ☐

NUMBER   YOUR
CORRECT   SCORE

IDENTIFY STORY ELEMENTS. The following questions check your knowledge of story elements. Put an *x* in the box next to each correct answer.

1. What happened last in the *plot* of "The Bet"?
   - ☐ a. A lively argument erupted at a dinner party.
   - ☐ b. The prisoner climbed through a window and ran off.
   - ☐ c. The banker decided to murder the prisoner.

2. Where is the story *set*?
   - ☐ a. in Russia more than one hundred years ago
   - ☐ b. in the United States
   - ☐ c. in France about twenty years ago

3. Which statement best expresses the *theme* of "The Bet"?
   - ☐ a. A man discovers over a period of time that there are things in life that are more meaningful than money.
   - ☐ b. To be happy, one must be wealthy.
   - ☐ c. Time passes very slowly if you do not have a radio or a television set.

4. The *conflict* between the banker and the lawyer arises from
   - ☐ a. a fight over honor.
   - ☐ b. the fact that they had been rivals since their youth.
   - ☐ c. differences in ideas and values.

NOTE WORDS IN A PASSAGE. The following questions use the cloze technique to check your reading comprehension. Complete the paragraph by filling in each blank with one of the words listed below. Each word appears in the story. Since there are five words and four blanks, one of the words will not be used.

"Stone walls do not a prison make,/Nor iron bars a cage." The poet Richard Lovelace wrote those stirring and _____ words more than 350 years ago. The lines of _____ suggest that even though a person may be locked in _____ , it is not really possible to lock up a person's thoughts. The poem is about the _____ of feeling and thought.

freedom   interesting

prison

obliged   poetry

☐ × 5 = ☐

NUMBER CORRECT   YOUR SCORE

☐ × 5 = ☐

NUMBER CORRECT   YOUR SCORE

117

KNOW HOW TO READ CRITICALLY. The following questions check your critical thinking skills. Put an *x* in the box next to each correct answer.

1. By purposely leaving the cottage early, the prisoner demonstrated that
   ☐ a. he was not interested in worldly goods.
   ☐ b. he couldn't wait to see his family.
   ☐ c. the death penalty is a kinder punishment than life in prison.

2. We may infer that the banker
   ☐ a. told all his friends about the prisoner's last letter.
   ☐ b. did not discuss the prisoner's last letter.
   ☐ c. gave the lawyer the money.

3. The banker's actions at the end of the story suggest that he
   ☐ a. thought that the lawyer was planning to borrow money from him.
   ☐ b. had lost respect for the lawyer.
   ☐ c. realized that the prisoner was a nobler and more honorable person than he.

4. Which statement is true?
   ☐ a. Although he was locked up for many years, the prisoner was never lonely.
   ☐ b. At the beginning of the story, the banker was quite worried that he would lose the bet.
   ☐ c. The banker's plan to kill the prisoner seems like the act of a desperate man.

☐ × 5 = ☐

NUMBER CORRECT   YOUR SCORE

Thinking for Writing and Discussion

- Over the course of years, the lawyer changed greatly in body and mind. Present evidence to support that statement.
- The banker believed that suspicion for the murder of the prisoner would fall on the watchman. Do you think that would really have happened? Explain your answer.
- Suppose the banker and the lawyer met each other ten years later. What do you think each might have said to the other?

Use the boxes below to total your scores for the exercises.

☐ **T**ELL ABOUT THE STORY
+
☐ **H**ANDLE NEW VOCABULARY WORDS
+
☐ **I**DENTIFY STORY ELEMENTS
+
☐ **N**OTE WORDS IN A PASSAGE
+
☐ **K**NOW HOW TO READ CRITICALLY
▼
☐ **Total Score:** Story 11

12. Ta-Na-E-Ka

by Mary Whitebird

As my birthday drew closer, I had awful nightmares about it. I was reaching the age at which all Kaw Indians had to participate in Ta-Na-E-Ka. Well, not all Kaws. Many of the younger families on the reservation were beginning to give up the old customs. But my grandfather, Amos Deer Leg, was devoted to tradition. He still wore handmade beaded moccasins instead of shoes, and kept his iron gray hair in tight braids. He could speak English, but he spoke it only with white men. With his family he used a Sioux dialect.

Grandfather was one of the last living Indians (he died when he was eighty-one) who actually fought against the U.S. Cavalry. Not only did he fight, he was wounded in a skirmish at Rose Creek—a famous encounter in which the celebrated Kaw chief Flat Nose lost his life. At the time, my grandfather was only eleven years old.

Eleven was a magic word among the Kaws. It was the time of Ta-Na-E-Ka, the "flowering of adulthood." It was the age, my grandfather

Meet the Kaw

The Kaw (or Kansa) Indians lived in the eastern and central parts of what is now called Kansas. A proud people strongly devoted to family traditions, they chose their chiefs for their courage, wisdom, and leadership ability. At one time the Kaw numbered in the thousands, but over the years smallpox and other diseases took a heavy toll. Fewer than six hundred Kaw survive today, and most of them live in Oklahoma.

119

informed us hundreds of times, "when a boy could prove himself to be a warrior and a girl took the first steps to womanhood."

"I don't want to be a warrior," my cousin, Roger Deer Leg, confided to me. "I'm going to become an accountant."

"None of the other tribes make girls go through the endurance ritual," I complained to my mother.

"It won't be as bad as you think, Mary," my mother said, ignoring my protests. "Once you've gone through it, you'll certainly never forget it. You'll be proud."

I even complained to my teacher, Mrs. Richardson, feeling that, as a white woman, she would side with me.

She didn't. "All of us have rituals of one kind or another," Mrs. Richardson said. "Don't look down on your heritage."

Heritage, indeed! I had no intention of living on a reservation for the rest of my life.

I've always thought that the Kaw were the originators of the women's liberation movement. No other Indian tribe treated women more equally than the Kaw. Unlike most of the subtribes of the Sioux Nation, the Kaw allowed men and women to eat together. And hundreds of years before we were "acculturated," a Kaw woman had the right to refuse a prospective husband even if her father arranged the match.

The wisest women (generally wisdom was equated with age) often sat in tribal councils. Furthermore, most Kaw legends revolve around "Good Woman." Good Woman led Kaw warriors into battle after battle from which they always seemed to emerge victorious.

Girls as well as boys were required to undergo Ta-Na-E-Ka. The actual ceremony varied from tribe to tribe, but since the Indians' life on the plains was dedicated to

survival, Ta-Na-E-Ka was a test of survival.

"Endurance is the loftiest virtue of the Indian," my grandfather explained. "To survive, we must endure. When I was a boy, Ta-Na-E-Ka was more than the mere symbol it is now. We were painted white with the juice of a sacred herb and sent naked into the wilderness without so much as a knife. We couldn't return until the white had worn off. It wouldn't wash off. It took almost eighteen days, and during that time we had to stay alive, trapping food, eating insects and roots and berries, and watching out for enemies. And we did have enemies—both the white soldiers and the Omaha warriors, who were always trying to capture Kaw boys and girls undergoing their endurance test. It was an exciting time."

"What happened if you couldn't make it?" Roger asked. He was born only three days after I was, and we were being trained for Ta-Na-E-Ka together. I was happy to know he was frightened, too.

"Many didn't return," Grandfather said. "Only the strongest and shrewdest. Mothers were not allowed to weep over those who didn't return. If a Kaw couldn't survive, he or she wasn't worth weeping over. It was our way."

"What a lot of hooey," Roger whispered. "I'd give anything to get out of it."

"I don't see how we have any choice," I replied.

Roger gave my arm a little squeeze. "Well, it's only five days."

Five days! Maybe it was better than being painted white and sent out naked for eighteen days. But not much better.

We were to be sent, barefoot and in bathing suits, into the woods. Even our very traditional parents put their foot down when Grandfather suggested we go naked. For five days we'd have to live off the land, keeping warm as best we could, getting food where we could. It was May, but on the northernmost reaches of the Missouri River the days were still chilly and the nights were fiercely cold.

Grandfather was in charge of the month's training for Ta-Na-E-Ka. One day he caught a grasshopper and demonstrated how to swallow it.

I felt sick, and Roger turned green. I told Roger teasingly, "You'd make a terrible warrior." Roger just grimaced.

I knew one thing. This particular Kaw Indian girl wasn't going to swallow a grasshopper no matter how hungry she got. And then I had an idea. Why hadn't I thought of it before? It would have saved nights of bad dreams about squooshy grasshoppers.

I headed straight for my teacher's house. "Mrs. Richardson," I said, "would you lend me five dollars?"

"Five dollars!" she exclaimed. "What for?"

"You remember the ceremony I talked about?"

"Ta-Na-E-Ka. Of course. Your parents have written me and asked me to excuse you from school so you can participate in it."

"Well, I need some things for the ceremony," I replied, in a half-truth. "I don't want to ask my parents for the money."

"It's not a crime to borrow money, Mary. But how can you pay it back?"

"I'll baby-sit for you."

"That's fair," she said, going to her purse and handing me a crisp, new, five-dollar bill.

"I'm happy to know the money's going to be put to good use," Mrs. Richardson said.

A few days later, the ritual began with a long speech from my grandfather about how we had reached the age of decision, how we now had to fend for ourselves and prove

that we could survive the most horrendous of ordeals. All the friends and relatives who had gathered at our house for dinner made jokes about their own Ta-Na-E-Ka experiences. They all advised us to fill up now, since for the next five days we'd be gorging ourselves on crickets. Neither Roger nor I was very hungry. "I'll probably laugh about this when I'm an accountant," Roger said, trembling.

"Are you trembling?" I asked.

"What do you think?"

"I'm happy to know boys tremble, too," I said.

At six the next morning we kissed our parents and went off to the woods. "Which side do you want?" Roger asked. According to the rules, Roger and I would stake out "territories" in separate areas of the woods and we weren't to communicate during the entire ordeal.

"I'll go toward the river, if it's okay with you," I said.

"Sure," Roger answered. "What difference does it make?"

To me, it made a lot of difference. There was a marina a few miles up the river and there were boats moored there. At least, I hoped so. I figured that a boat was a better place to sleep than under a pile of leaves.

"Why do you keep holding your head?" Roger asked.

"Oh, nothing. Just nervous," I told him. Actually, I was afraid I'd lose the five-dollar bill, which I had tucked into my hair with a bobby pin. As we came to a fork in the trail, Roger shook my hand. "Good luck, Mary."

"N'ko-n'ta," I said. It was the Kaw word for *courage*.

The sun was shining and it was warm, but my bare feet began to hurt immediately. I spied one of the berry bushes Grandfather had told us about. "You're lucky," he had said. "The berries are ripe in the spring, and they are delicious and nourishing." They were orange and fat and I popped one into my mouth.

Argh! I spat it out. It was awful and bitter, and even grasshoppers were probably better tasting, although I never intended to find out.

I sat down to rest my feet. A rabbit hopped out from under the berry bush. He nuzzled the berry I'd spat out and ate it. He picked another one and ate that, too. He liked them. He looked at me, twitching his nose. I watched a red-headed woodpecker bore into an elm tree, and I caught a glimpse of a civet cat waddling through some twigs. All of a sudden I realized I was no longer frightened. Ta-Na-E-Ka might be more fun than I'd anticipated. I got up and headed toward the marina.

"Not one boat," I said to myself dejectedly. But the restaurant on the shore, "Ernie's Riverside," was open. I walked in, feeling silly in my bathing suit. The man at the counter was big and tough-looking. He wore a sweatshirt with the words "Fort Sheridan" on it. He asked me what I wanted.

"A hamburger and a milk shake," I said, holding the five-dollar bill in my hand so he'd know I had money.

"That's a pretty heavy breakfast," he murmured.

"That's what I always have for breakfast," I lied.

"Forty-five cents," he said, bringing me the food. (Back then, hamburgers were twenty-five cents and milk shakes were twenty cents.) "Delicious," I thought. "Better'n grasshoppers—and Grandfather never once mentioned that I couldn't eat hamburgers."

While I was eating, I had a great idea. Why not sleep in the restaurant? I went to the ladies' room and made sure the window was unlocked. Then I went back outside and played along the riverbank, watching the water birds and trying to identify each one. I planned to look for a beaver dam the next day.

The restaurant closed at sunset, and I watched the man drive away. Then I climbed in the unlocked window. There was a night light on, so I didn't turn on any lights. But there was a radio on the counter. I turned it on to a music program. It was warm in the restaurant, and I was hungry. I helped myself to a glass of milk and a piece of pie, intending to keep a list of what I'd eaten so I could leave money. I also planned to get up early, sneak out through the window, and head for the woods before the counter man returned. I turned off the radio, wrapped myself in the man's apron, and, in spite of the hardness of the floor, fell asleep.

"What are you doing here, kid?"

It was the man's voice.

It was morning. I'd overslept. I was scared.

"Hold it, kid. I just wanna know what you're doing here. You lost? You must be from the reservation. Your folks must be worried sick about you. Do they have a phone?"

"Yes, yes," I answered. "But don't call them."

I was shivering. The man, who told me his name was Ernie, made me a cup of hot chocolate while I explained about Ta-Na-E-Ka.

"How do you like that?" he said, when I was through. "Lived next to the reservation all my life and this is the first I've heard of Ta-Na-whatever-you-call-it." He looked at me. "Pretty silly thing to do to a kid," he muttered.

That was just what I'd been thinking for months, but when Ernie said it, I became angry. "No, it isn't silly. It's a custom of the Kaw. We've been doing this for hundreds of years. My mother and my grandfather and everybody in my family went through this ceremony. It's why the Kaw are great warriors."

"Okay, great warrior," Ernie chuckled, "suit yourself. And, if you want to stick around, it's okay with me." Ernie went to the broom closet and tossed me a bundle. "That's the lost-and-found closet," he said. "Stuff people left on boats. Maybe there's something to keep you warm."

The sweater fitted loosely, but it felt good. I felt good. And I'd found a new friend. Most important, I was surviving Ta-Na-E-Ka.

My grandfather had said the experience would be filled with adventure, and I was having my fill. And Grandfather has never said we couldn't accept hospitality.

I stayed at Ernie's Riverside for the entire period. In the mornings I went into the woods and watched the animals and picked flowers for each of the tables in Ernie's. I had never felt better. I was up early enough to watch the sun rise on the Missouri, and I went to bed after it set. I ate everything I wanted—insisting that Ernie take all my money for the food. "I'll keep this in trust for you, Mary," Ernie promised, "in case you are ever desperate for five dollars."

I was sorry when the five days were over. I'd enjoyed every minute with Ernie. He taught me how to make western omelets and to make Chili Ernie Style (still one of my favorite dishes). And I told Ernie all about the legends of the Kaw. I hadn't realized I knew so much about my people.

Ta-Na-E-Ka was over, and as I approached my house, at about nine-thirty in the evening, I became nervous all over again. What if Grandfather asked me about the berries and the grasshoppers? And my feet were hardly cut. I hadn't lost a pound and my hair was combed. "They'll be so happy to see me," I told myself hopefully, "that they won't ask too many questions."

I opened the door. My grandfather was in the front room. He was wearing the ceremonial beaded deerskin shirt which had belonged to *his* grandfather. "N'g'da'ma," he said. "Welcome back."

I embraced my parents warmly, letting go only when I saw my cousin Roger sprawled on the couch. His eyes were red and swollen. He'd lost weight. His feet were an unsightly mass of blood and blisters, and he was moaning: "I made it, see. I made it. I'm a warrior. A warrior."

My grandfather looked at me strangely. I was clean, obviously well fed, and radiantly healthy. My parents got the message. My uncle and aunt gazed at me with hostility.

Finally my grandfather asked, "What did you eat to keep you so well?"

I sucked in my breath and blurted out the truth: "Hamburgers and milk shakes."

"Hamburgers!" my grandfather growled.

"Milk shakes!" Roger moaned.

"You didn't say we *had* to eat grasshoppers," I said sheepishly.

"Tell us about your Ta-Na-E-Ka," my grandfather commanded.

I told them everything, from borrowing the five dollars, to Ernie's kindness.

"That's not what I trained you for," my grandfather said sadly.

I stood up. "Grandfather, I learned that Ta-Na-E-Ka is important. I didn't think so during training. I was scared stiff of it. I handled it my way. And I learned I had nothing to be afraid of. There's no reason nowadays to eat grasshoppers when you can eat a hamburger."

I was inwardly shocked at my own audacity. But I liked it. "Grandfather, I'll bet you never ate one of those rotten berries yourself."

Grandfather laughed! He laughed aloud! My mother and father and aunt and uncle were all dumbfounded. Grandfather never laughed. Never.

"Those berries—they are terrible," Grandfather admitted. "I could never swallow them. I found a dead deer on the first day of my Ta-Na-E-Ka—shot by a soldier, probably— and he kept my belly full for the entire period of the test!"

I looked at Roger. "You're pretty smart, Mary," Roger groaned. "I'd never have thought of what you did."

Roger tried to smile, but couldn't. My grandfather called me to him. "You should have done what your cousin did. But I think you are more alert to what is happening to our people today than we are. I think you would have passed the test under any circumstances, in any time. Somehow, you know how to exist in a world that wasn't made for Indians. I don't think you're going to have any trouble surviving."

Grandfather wasn't entirely right. But I'll tell about that another time.

TELL ABOUT THE STORY. The following questions help you check your reading comprehension. Put an *x* in the box next to each correct answer.

1. As the time to participate in Ta-Na-E-Ka drew nearer, Mary and Roger felt
   ☐ a. calm.
   ☐ b. eager.
   ☐ c. frightened.

2. When she was at the restaurant, Mary told Ernie
   ☐ a. that she was lost and wanted to go home.
   ☐ b. about the legends of the Kaw.
   ☐ c. to call her parents and say she was safe.

3. Mary told her family that she had lived on
   ☐ a. berries and insects.
   ☐ b. hamburgers and milk shakes.
   ☐ c. fish that she caught.

4. At the end of the story, Mary's family was surprised because she
   ☐ a. had managed to survive her Ta-Na-E-Ka.
   ☐ b. had lost weight and was bruised and exhausted.
   ☐ c. looked clean, well fed, and healthy.

HANDLE NEW VOCABULARY WORDS. The following questions check your vocabulary skills. Put an *x* in the box next to each correct answer.

1. Grandfather said that in the spring the berries were ripe, delicious, and nourishing. Which expression best defines the word *nourishing*?
   ☐ a. difficult to find
   ☐ b. not very large
   ☐ c. good for keeping a person alive

2. Roger and Mary had to prove they could survive the ordeal of Ta-Na-E-Ka. What is an *ordeal*?
   ☐ a. an amusing incident
   ☐ b. a severe test or experience
   ☐ c. a pleasant surprise

3. Grandfather was wounded in a skirmish with the U.S. Cavalry. A *skirmish* is a
   ☐ a. fight.
   ☐ b. dance.
   ☐ c. journey.

4. Everyone was dumbfounded when Grandfather, who never laughed, laughed. The word *dumbfounded* means
   ☐ a. annoyed.
   ☐ b. amazed.
   ☐ c. relaxed.

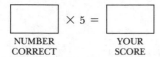

NUMBER CORRECT × 5 = YOUR SCORE

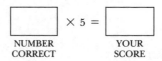

NUMBER CORRECT × 5 = YOUR SCORE

IDENTIFY STORY ELEMENTS. The following questions check your knowledge of story elements. Put an *x* in the box next to each correct answer.

1. Who is the *main character* of "Ta-Na-E-Ka"?
   ☐ a. Mary
   ☐ b. Roger
   ☐ c. Grandfather

2. What happened last in the *plot* of the story?
   ☐ a. Mary borrowed five dollars from Mrs. Richardson.
   ☐ b. Roger declared, "I made it. I'm a warrior."
   ☐ c. Grandfather demonstrated how to swallow a grasshopper.

3. Which word best *characterizes* Mary?
   ☐ a. cowardly
   ☐ b. independent
   ☐ c. shy

4. The *conflict* between Grandfather and Mary represents the struggle between
   ☐ a. family members who don't care about each other.
   ☐ b. two people who are very foolish.
   ☐ c. the old ways and the new ways.

NOTE WORDS IN A PASSAGE. The following questions use the cloze technique to check your reading comprehension. Complete the paragraph by filling in each blank with one of the words listed below. Each word appears in the story. Since there are five words and four blanks, one of the words will not be used.

When you take a camping trip, you must think about what food, clothing, and equipment will be _____ . Here are some tips from _____ campers. Always take a first-aid kit, and bring matches in a waterproof container. Under no _____ should you leave without a sufficient supply of water. Keep a hat on your head and wear long pants, since they _____ provide more protection than shorts.

experienced   circumstances

survival

required   obviously

☐ × 5 = ☐

NUMBER   YOUR
CORRECT   SCORE

☐ × 5 = ☐

NUMBER   YOUR
CORRECT   SCORE

KNOW HOW TO READ CRITICALLY. The following questions check your critical thinking skills. Put an *x* in the box next to each correct answer.

1. We may infer that Grandfather thought that Mary would return home looking
   - ☐ a. more rested than when she left.
   - ☐ b. exactly the same as when she left.
   - ☐ c. as though she had faced difficulty and hardship.

2. Clues in the story suggest that Ernie was
   - ☐ a. angry with Mary for falling asleep in the restaurant.
   - ☐ b. bored with what Mary told him about the Kaw.
   - ☐ c. very concerned about Mary's welfare.

3. Which statement is true?
   - ☐ a. Their methods were different, but Roger and Mary each proved that they could survive.
   - ☐ b. Roger refused to talk to Mary because he thought she had cheated during her Ta-Na-E-Ka.
   - ☐ c. Mary told Ernie that the customs of the Kaw were silly.

4. Although Grandfather was not happy about the way Mary handled her Ta-Na-E-Ka, he believed that she
   - ☐ a. told the truth and therefore should not be criticized for her actions.
   - ☐ b. demonstrated the ability to deal effectively with today's world.
   - ☐ c. couldn't have acted any other way.

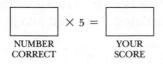

NUMBER CORRECT × 5 = YOUR SCORE

Thinking for Writing and Discussion

- Although Mary's Ta-Na-E-Ka was different and unique, it was certainly a worthwhile learning experience for her. Do you agree or disagree with that statement? Support your opinion.
- In defending her actions, Mary made the following statements:
  "Grandfather never once mentioned that I couldn't eat hamburgers."
  " 'You didn't say we *had* to eat grasshoppers.' "
  ". . . Grandfather has never said we couldn't accept hospitality."
  Support or attack Mary's reasoning.
- According to Grandfather, Mary "would have passed the test under any circumstances." What did Grandfather mean? Why do you think he drew that conclusion? Do you agree with him? Explain.

Use the boxes below to total your scores for the exercises.

☐ **T**ELL ABOUT THE STORY
   +
☐ **H**ANDLE NEW VOCABULARY WORDS
   +
☐ **I**DENTIFY STORY ELEMENTS
   +
☐ **N**OTE WORDS IN A PASSAGE
   +
☐ **K**NOW HOW TO READ CRITICALLY
   ▼
☐ **Total Score:** Story 12

13. All Summer in a Day

by Ray Bradbury

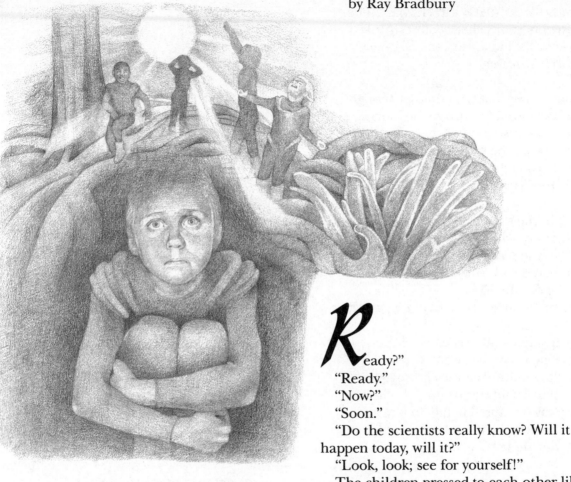

Meet the Author

Ray Bradbury (1920–   ) is probably today's leading writer of science fiction and fantasy. Born in Waukegan, Illinois, Bradbury eventually moved to Los Angeles, which continues to be his home. He has written many short stories, novels, and radio, television, and motion-picture scripts. His short-story collections include *The Martian Chronicles* and *The Illustrated Man.* His best-known novel, *Fahrenheit 451,* is about a frightening book-burning society of the future.

"Keady?"

"Ready."

"Now?"

"Soon."

"Do the scientists really know? Will it happen today, will it?"

"Look, look; see for yourself!"

The children pressed to each other like so many roses, so many weeds, intermixed,[1] peering out for a look at the hidden sun.

It rained.

It had been raining for seven years; thousands upon thousands of days compounded and filled from one end to the other with rain, with the drum and gush of water, with the sweet crystal fall of showers and the concussion of storms so heavy they were tidal waves come over the islands. A thousand forests had been crushed under the rain and grown up a

_____

1. **intermixed:** mixed together.

thousand times to be crushed again. And this was the way life was forever on the planet Venus, and this was the schoolroom of the children of the rocket men and women who had come to a raining world to set up civilization and live out their lives.

"It's stopping, it's stopping!"

"Yes, yes!"

Margot stood apart from them, from these children who could never remember a time when there wasn't rain and rain and rain. They were all nine years old, and if there had been a day, seven years ago, when the sun came out for an hour and showed its face to the stunned world, they could not recall. Sometimes, at night, she heard them stir, in remembrance, and she knew they were dreaming and remembering gold or a yellow crayon or a coin large enough to buy the world with. She knew they thought they remembered a warmness, like a blushing in the face, in the body, in the arms and legs and trembling hands. But then they always awoke to the tatting drum, the endless shaking down of clear bead necklaces upon the roof, the walk, the gardens, the forests, and their dreams were gone.

All day yesterday they had read in class about the sun. About how like a lemon it was, and how hot. And they had written small stories or essays or poems about it:

I think the sun is a flower,
That blooms for just one hour.

That was Margot's poem, read in a quiet voice in the still classroom while the rain was falling outside.

"Aw, you didn't write that!" protested one of the boys.

"I did," said Margot, "I *did*."

"William!" said the teacher.

But that was yesterday. Now the rain was slackening, and the children were crushed in the great thick windows.

"Where's teacher?"

"She'll be back."

"She'd better hurry, we'll miss it!"

They turned on themselves, like a feverish wheel, all tumbling spokes.

Margot stood alone. She was a very frail girl who looked as if she had been lost in the rain for years and the rain had washed out the blue from her eyes and the red from her mouth and the yellow from her hair. She was an old photograph dusted from an album, whitened away, and if she spoke at all her voice would be a ghost. Now she stood, separate, staring at the rain and the loud wet world beyond the huge glass.

"What're *you* looking at?" said William.

Margot said nothing.

"Speak when you're spoken to." He gave her a shove. But she did not move; rather she let herself be moved only by him and nothing else.

They edged away from her, they would not look at her. She felt them go away. And this was because she would play no games with them in the echoing tunnels of the underground city. If they tagged her and ran, she stood blinking after them and did not follow. When the class sang songs about happiness and life and games her lips barely moved. Only when they sang about the sun and the summer did her lips move as she watched the drenched windows.

And then, of course, the biggest crime of all was that she had come here only five years ago from Earth, and she remembered the sun and the way the sun was and the sky was when she was four in Ohio. And they, they had been on Venus all their lives, and they had been only two years old when last the sun came out and had long since forgotten the color and heat of it and the way it really was. But Margot remembered.

"It's like a penny," she said once, eyes closed.

"No it's not!" the children cried.

"It's like a fire," she said, "in the stove."

"You're lying, you don't remember!" cried the children.

But she remembered and stood quietly apart from all of them and watched the patterning windows. And once, a month ago, she had refused to shower in the school shower rooms, had clutched her hands to her ears and over her head, screaming the water musn't touch her head. So after that, dimly, dimly, she sensed it, she was different and they knew her difference and kept away.

There was talk that her father and mother were taking her back to Earth next year; it seemed vital to her that they do so, though it would mean the loss of thousands of dollars to her family. And so, the children hated her for all these reasons of big and little consequence. They hated her pale snow face, her waiting silence, her thinness, and her possible future.

"Get away!" The boy gave her another push. "What're you waiting for?"

Then, for the first time, she turned and looked at him. And what she was waiting for was in her eyes.

"Well, don't wait around here!" cried the boy savagely. "You won't see nothing!"

Her lips moved.

"Nothing!" he cried. "It was all a joke, wasn't it?" He turned to the other children. "Nothing's happening today. Is it?"

They all blinked at him and then, understanding, laughed and shook their heads. "Nothing, nothing!"

"Oh, but," Margot whispered, her eyes helpless. "But this is the day, the scientists predict, they say, they know, the sun . . ."

"All a joke!" said the boy, and seized her roughly. "Hey, everyone, let's put her in a closet before teacher comes!"

"No," said Margot, falling back.

They surged about her, caught her up and bore her, protesting, and then pleading, and then crying, back into a tunnel, a room, a closet, where they slammed and locked the door. They stood looking at the door and saw it tremble from her beating and throwing herself against it. They heard her muffled cries. Then, smiling, they turned and went out and back down the tunnel, just as the teacher arrived.

"Ready, children?" She glanced at her watch.

"Yes!" said everyone.

"Are we all here?"

"Yes!"

The rain slackened still more.

They crowded to the huge door.

The rain stopped.

It was as if, in the midst of a film, concerning an avalanche, a tornado, a hurricane, a volcanic eruption, something had, first, gone wrong with the sound apparatus, thus muffling and finally cutting off all noise, all of the blasts and repercussions and thunders, and then, second, ripped the film from the projector and inserted in its place a peaceful tropical slide which did not move or tremor. The world ground to a standstill. The silence was so immense and unbelievable that you felt your ears had been stuffed or you had lost your hearing altogether. The children put their hands to their ears. They stood apart. The door slid back and the smell of the silent, waiting world came in to them.

The sun came out.

It was the color of flaming bronze and it

was very large. And the sky around it was a blazing blue tile color. And the jungle burned with sunlight as the children, released from their spell, rushed out, yelling, into the springtime.

"Now, don't go too far," called the teacher after them. "You've only two hours, you know. You wouldn't want to get caught out!"

But they were running and turning their faces up to the sky and feeling the sun on their cheeks like a warm iron; they were taking off their jackets and letting the sun burn their arms.

"Oh, it's better than the sunlamps, isn't it?"

"Much, much better!"

They stopped running and stood in the great jungle that covered Venus, that grew and never stopped growing, tumultuously, even as you watched it. It was a nest of octopi, clustering up great arms of fleshlike weed, wavering, flowering this brief spring. It was the color of rubber and ash, this jungle, from the many years without sun. It was the color of stones and white cheeses and ink, and it was the color of the moon.

The children lay out, laughing, on the jungle mattress, and heard it sigh and squeak under them, resilient[2] and alive. They ran among the trees, they slipped and fell, they pushed each other, they played hide-and-seek and tag, but most of all they squinted at the sun until the tears ran down their faces, they put their hands up to that yellowness and that amazing blueness and they breathed of the fresh, fresh air and listened and listened to the silence which suspended them in a blessed sea of no sound and no motion. They looked at everything and savored[3] everything.

Then, wildly, like animals escaped from their caves, they ran and ran in shouting circles. They ran for an hour and did not stop running.

And then—

In the midst of their running one of the girls wailed.

Everyone stopped.

The girl, standing in the open, held out her hand.

"Oh, look, look," she said, trembling.

They came slowly to look at her opened palm.

In the center of it, cupped and huge, was a single raindrop.

She began to cry, looking at it.

They glanced quietly at the sky.

"Oh. Oh."

A few cold drops fell on their noses and their cheeks and their mouths. The sun faded behind a stir of mist. A wind blew cool around them. They turned and started to walk back toward the underground house, their hands at their sides, their smiles vanishing away.

A boom of thunder startled them and like leaves before a new hurricane, they tumbled upon each other and ran. Lightning struck ten miles away, five miles away, a mile, a half mile. The sky darkened into midnight in a flash.

They stood in the doorway of the underground for a moment until it was raining hard. Then they closed the door and heard the gigantic sound of the rain falling in tons and avalanches, everywhere and forever.

"Will it be seven more years?"

"Yes. Seven."

Then one of them gave a little cry.

"Margot!"

"What?"

"She's still in the closet where we locked her."

"Margot."

They stood as if someone had driven them,

---

2. **resilient:** able to spring back after being stretched or bent.
3. **savored:** took great pleasure in; enjoyed very much.

like so many stakes, into the floor. They looked at each other and then looked away. They glanced out at the world that was raining now and raining and raining steadily. They could not meet each other's glances. Their faces were solemn and pale. They looked at their hands and feet, their faces down.

"Margot."

One of the girls said, "Well. . . ?"

No one moved.

"Go on," whispered the girl.

They walked slowly down the hall in the sound of cold rain. They turned through the doorway to the room in the sound of the storm and thunder, lightning on their faces, blue and terrible. They walked over to the closet door slowly and stood by it.

Behind the closet door was only silence.

They unlocked the door, even more slowly, and let Margot out.

TELL ABOUT THE STORY. The following questions help you check your reading comprehension. Put an *x* in the box next to each correct answer.

1. Margot's biggest crime was that she
   ☐ a. always bragged about herself.
   ☐ b. wrote the best poems in the class.
   ☐ c. came from Earth and remembered the sky and the sun.

2. The children ran and shouted in the sun for
   ☐ a. an hour.
   ☐ b. the entire afternoon.
   ☐ c. most of the day.

3. By the time the children remembered that Margot was in the closet, it was
   ☐ a. time to have lunch.
   ☐ b. already raining hard.
   ☐ c. time to go home.

4. At the conclusion of the story, the children
   ☐ a. released Margot.
   ☐ b. questioned Margot.
   ☐ c. teased Margot some more.

HANDLE NEW VOCABULARY WORDS. The following questions check your vocabulary skills. Put an *x* in the box next to each correct answer.

1. The rain slackened and finally stopped. The word *slackened* means
   ☐ a. froze.
   ☐ b. increased.
   ☐ c. became slower.

2. The children surged around Margot and finally caught her. Define the word *surged*.
   ☐ a. rushed; swept like a wave
   ☐ b. retreated; went away from
   ☐ c. praised; approved of

3. The great jungle that covered Venus never stopped growing; it grew violently, tumultuously. Which of the following words best defines *tumultuously*?
   ☐ a. wildly
   ☐ b. peacefully
   ☐ c. happily

4. The students stood without moving, like stakes driven into the ground. As used here, the word *stakes* means
   ☐ a. money.
   ☐ b. sticks.
   ☐ c. portions.

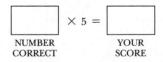

	× 5 =	
NUMBER CORRECT		YOUR SCORE

	× 5 =	
NUMBER CORRECT		YOUR SCORE

IDENTIFY STORY ELEMENTS. The following questions check your knowledge of story elements. Put an *x* in the box next to each correct answer.

1. What is the *setting* of "All Summer in a Day"?
   ☐ a. Venus some time in the future
   ☐ b. Earth fifty years from now
   ☐ c. the moon at the present time

2. What happened last in the *plot* of the story?
   ☐ a. The rain stopped.
   ☐ b. The children let Margot out of the closet.
   ☐ c. William gave Margot a shove.

3. What is the *mood* of "All Summer in a Day"?
   ☐ a. cheerful
   ☐ b. humorous
   ☐ c. frightening

4. The *conflict* in the story stems from the fact that the children
   ☐ a. were much older than Margot.
   ☐ b. were better athletes than Margot.
   ☐ c. considered Margot to be different from them.

NOTE WORDS IN A PASSAGE. The following questions use the cloze technique to check your reading comprehension. Complete the paragraph by filling in each blank with one of the words listed below. Each word appears in the story. Since there are five words and four blanks, one of the words will not be used.

When they must describe a _____ 1

on a distant planet, authors tend to write

about Venus and Mars. Authors may choose

those planets because, in our _____ 2

solar system, Venus and Mars are the easiest

planets to see. According to _____ , 3

Venus is the brightest planet. But Mars also

appeals to writers because its bright

_____ color makes it easy to 4

detect in the sky.

immense   civilization

scientists

predict   red

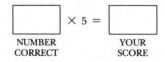

NUMBER CORRECT × 5 = YOUR SCORE

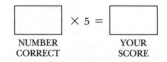

NUMBER CORRECT × 5 = YOUR SCORE

KNOW HOW TO READ CRITICALLY. The following questions check your critical thinking skills. Put an *x* in the box next to each correct answer.

1. In "All Summer in a Day," the author, Ray Bradbury, suggests that
   - ☐ a. it is usually bright and sunny on Venus.
   - ☐ b. it rains almost all the time on Venus.
   - ☐ c. the inhabitants of Venus are very happy people.

2. Which statement is false?
   - ☐ a. Of all the children, only Margot remembered the sun.
   - ☐ b. None of the children had been born on Venus.
   - ☐ c. Margot might be returning to Earth next year.

3. At the end of the story the children could not look at each other, but looked down with faces solemn and pale. Their behavior indicates that the children were
   - ☐ a. ashamed of what they had done.
   - ☐ b. glad they had punished Margot.
   - ☐ c. wondering what the next day's weather would be.

4. Clues in the story suggest that the children were
   - ☐ a. jealous of Margot.
   - ☐ b. smarter than Margot.
   - ☐ c. wealthier than Margot.

☐ × 5 = ☐

NUMBER CORRECT   YOUR SCORE

Thinking for Writing and Discussion

- Why do you think Ray Bradbury called this story "All Summer in a Day"? Make up another title that would also be appropriate.
- To create a picture in the reader's mind, Bradbury uses similes—comparisons that use the words *like* or *as*. For example, the sun was *like* a warm iron, and the children pressed against each other *like* roses. Using the words *like* or *as*, make up two similes of your own. In your first simile, describe the sun. In your second simile, describe the children.
- In a sense, "All Summer in a Day" is a story about prejudice. Present evidence from the story to support that statement.

Use the boxes below to total your scores for the exercises.

☐ **T**ELL ABOUT THE STORY
+
☐ **H**ANDLE NEW VOCABULARY WORDS
+
☐ **I**DENTIFY STORY ELEMENTS
+
☐ **N**OTE WORDS IN A PASSAGE
+
☐ **K**NOW HOW TO READ CRITICALLY
▼
☐ **Total Score:** Story 13

14. Love of Life

by Jack London

They limped painfully down the bank of the stream, making their way among the jagged rocks. They were tired and weak, and their faces had the weary expression which comes from hardships long endured. Both men had packs strapped to their shoulders. Both carried a rifle. They walked stooped over, shoulders forward, eyes bent upon the ground.

"I wish we had a few of those bullets we left back in camp," said one of the two men. His voice was dreary and expressionless. He spoke without enthusiasm.

The other man, following at his heels, did not answer. The men made their way through the water which was icy cold—so cold that their ankles ached and their feet went numb. The water foamed over the rocks and splashed up against their knees, and both men staggered, trying to keep their footing.

The second of the two men slipped on a smooth rock and nearly fell; but he recovered with a violent effort, uttering a loud cry of pain as he did. For a moment he seemed dizzy and

Meet the Author

Jack London (1876–1916) was born in San Francisco. He traveled widely, living a life as exciting as those of the many characters he created. Lured by the prospect of discovering gold, London set out for the Yukon in 1897. The experience enriched his life and provided the background for his world-famous novels, *The Call of the Wild* and *White Fang*. "Love of Life" and "To Build a Fire" are two of London's best-known short stories.

faint. He thrust out his hand as though trying to use the air for balance and support. After he had steadied himself he stepped forward, but slipped again and nearly fell. Then he stood still. He looked at the other man who had never turned his head.

For a full moment the man stood still, as though debating with himself. Then he called out, "Hey, Bill! Bill! I've sprained my ankle."

But Bill continued to stagger on through the foaming water. He did not turn around. The injured man watched him go, and though his face showed no expression, his eyes were like the eyes of a wounded deer.

Bill continued straight on without looking back. The other man watched him. His lips trembled a little.

"Bill!" he cried out.

It was the pleading cry of a strong man in distress, but Bill's head did not turn. The injured man watched him lurch forward up the slope toward the soft skyline of the low-lying hill. He watched him go till Bill passed over the crest and disappeared. Then the injured man turned his gaze and slowly took in the circle of the world that remained to him now that Bill was gone.

Near the horizon the sky was smoldering dimly, its light almost obscured by drifting mists and vapors. The man pulled out his watch while resting his weight on one leg. It was four o'clock, and it was the last week of July or the first week of August—he did not know the precise date. He looked to the south and knew that somewhere beyond those bleak hills lay the Great Bear Lake. He knew that the stream in which he stood fed the Coppermine River, which flowed north and emptied into the Arctic Ocean. He had never been there, but he had seen it once, on a Hudson Bay Trading Company map.

Again his gaze took in the circle of the world about him. It was not an encouraging sight. Everywhere there was the skyline with low-lying hills. There were no trees, no shrubs, no grasses, nothing but a tremendous and terrible wilderness—a desolate emptiness that sent fear swiftly into his eyes.

"Bill!" he whispered once, and then again, "Bill!"

He bent over in the midst of the rushing water, as though the vastness was pressing in on him with overwhelming force, brutally crushing him. He suddenly began to shake, as though he had a fever, until the rifle fell from his hand with a splash. This served to rouse him. He fought his fear and pulled himself together, and groped in the water until he had recovered the weapon. He hitched his pack farther back over his left shoulder to take some of its weight off his injured ankle. Then he proceeded, slowly and carefully, wincing with pain as he went.

He did not stop. Madly, desperately, disregarding the pain, he hurried up the slope toward the top of the hill over which Bill had disappeared. But at the top he looked down into a valley which was empty of life. He fought with his fever again, overcame it, hitched the pack still farther over his left shoulder, and lurched on down the slope.

The bottom of the valley was soggy with wet moss. At every step water squirted out from under his feet, and each time he lifted a foot he heard a sucking sound as the wet moss slowly and reluctantly released its grip. He picked his way along, following Bill's footsteps through the sea of moss.

Though alone, he was not lost. Farther on, he knew, he would come to a place of dead spruce and fir trees. This place was called the "land of little sticks," and it bordered a small lake. A stream flowed into the lake. He would follow that stream to another stream which flowed west and emptied into the Dease River. There he would find a cache, a hiding place, under an upturned canoe piled over with many rocks. And in this hiding place would be ammunition for his empty gun, fishhooks and lines, a small net—everything he needed for killing and snaring food. Also, he would find flour, a piece of bacon, and some beans.

Bill would be waiting for him there at the cache, and they would paddle south down the Dease River to the Great Bear Lake. And south across the lake they would go, ever south, south, while the winter raced vainly after them, and the ice formed, and the days grew chill and crisp, south to the warm Hudson Bay Company post where there were friends waiting and there was food without end.

These were the thoughts of the man as he made his way onward. All the while he tried to think that Bill had not deserted him, that Bill would surely wait for him at the hiding place. He was compelled to think this thought, or there would have been no reason to push on, and he would have fallen down and died. So, over and over, he thought of the food at the cache and of Bill waiting for him there.

Meanwhile, he had not eaten for two days. So he stooped as he went and picked pale muskeg berries, put them into his mouth and chewed and swallowed them. A muskeg berry is a bit of seed enclosed in a bit of water. In the mouth the water melts away and the seed tastes sharp and bitter. The man knew there was no nourishment in the berries, but he chewed them patiently anyway.

At nine o'clock he stubbed his toe on a rocky ledge, and from sheer weakness and weariness, he staggered and fell. He lay on his side for some time without moving. Then he slipped off the straps of his pack and clumsily dragged himself to a sitting position. It was not yet dark, and in the lingering twilight he groped about among the rocks for shreds of dry moss. When he had gathered a heap he built a fire—a smoldering, smudgy fire—and put on a tin pot of water to boil.

He unwrapped his pack and the first thing he did was to count his matches. There were sixty-seven. He counted them twice to make sure. Then he divided them into three packs, wrapping them carefully in oil paper. He put one bunch in his pack, another bunch in the inside band of his battered hat, and the third bunch under his shirt on his chest. This accomplished, a panic came over him, and he unwrapped them all and counted them again. There were still sixty-seven.

He dried his wet footgear by the fire. The moccasins were soggy and shredded. The socks were worn through in places, and his feet were raw and bleeding. His ankle was throbbing, and he now examined it. It had swollen to the size of his knee. He tore a long strip from one of his two blankets and wrapped the strip around the ankle tightly. He tore other strips and wrapped them around his feet to serve as both moccasins and socks. Then he drank the pot of water, steaming hot, wound his watch, and crawled between his blankets.

He slept like a dead man.

At six o'clock he awoke, lying on his back. He gazed straight up into the gray sky and was seized by pangs of hunger. As he rolled over on his elbow, he was startled by a loud snort, and saw a caribou staring at him with alert curiosity. The animal was not more than fifty feet away, and instantly into the man's mind there leaped the vision of caribou steak sizzling over a fire. Without a second thought he reached for the empty gun, took aim, and pulled the trigger. The caribou leaped away, his hoofs rattling as he fled.

The man cursed and flung the empty gun away from him. He groaned as he dragged himself to his feet. It was a slow and difficult task. His joints were like rusty hinges, and it was several minutes before he could stand up.

He crawled up a small hill and looked around. There were no trees, no bushes, nothing but gray everywhere. The moss was gray, the sky gray. There was no sun or hint of sun. He had no idea where north was, and had forgotten the way he had come to this spot the night before. But he was not lost. He knew that. Soon he would come to the land of the little sticks. He felt certain that it lay somewhere off to the left, not far, possibly just over the next low hill.

He went back to put his pack into shape for traveling. First he made sure that he had his three packs of matches, though this time he did not stop to count them. However, for a long time he debated over a small leather sack in his pack. This sack was not large, but it weighed fifteen pounds, as much as the rest of his pack—and it worried him. He thought about this sack for a long time, and when he finally rose to stagger on, it was included in his pack.

He made his way to the left, stopping now and then to eat muskeg berries. His ankle had stiffened and his limp was worse, but the pain in it was nothing compared to the pain in his stomach. The hunger pangs were so sharp that it was hard to keep his mind on the course he must travel.

He came into a valley whose rocky ledges were filled with birds. *Ker—ker—ker* was the cry they made. How good they would be for food, he thought. He threw stones at them, but he could not hit them. He placed his pack on the ground and stalked them the way a cat stalks a sparrow. The sharp rocks cut through his pants legs till his knees left a trail of blood, but his hunger was so great he could not feel the hurt. Always the birds flew higher, mocking him with their *ker—ker—ker,* and he cursed and cried aloud because he could not catch them.

As the day wore on, a band of caribou passed by, twenty of them. So tantalizing they were—within rifle shot, but out of reach. A black fox came toward him, carrying a bird in its mouth. The man shouted loudly. It was a horrible, blood-curdling cry; but the fox leaped away in fright and did not drop the bird.

As he pushed on, he looked vainly into every pool of water he saw until, as twilight came on, he discovered a fish, the size of a minnow, in such a pool. He plunged his arm in up to the shoulder, but the fish eluded him. He reached for it with both hands and stirred up the mud at the bottom. In his excitement he fell in, drenching himself to the waist. Then the water was too muddy to permit him to see the fish, and he was compelled to wait until the sediment had settled.

Finally he renewed the pursuit. He unwrapped the tin bucket and began to bail the pool. He bailed wildly at first, splashing himself with water. He tried to be more careful, though his heart was pounding against his chest, and his hands were trembling. At the end of half an hour, the pool was nearly dry. Not a cupful of water remained. And there was no fish. It had found a hidden crevice among the stones through which it had escaped to the adjoining and larger pool—a pool which the man could not empty in a night and a day. Had he known of the crevice, he could have closed it with a rock at the beginning and the fish would have been his.

He sank down upon the wet earth and cried softly to himself, and, for a long time after, he was shaken by great sobs.

He built a fire and warmed himself by drinking quarts of hot water, and then made camp on a rocky ledge the same way he had the night before. The last thing he did was to make sure that his matches were dry and to wind his watch. The blankets were wet and clammy and his ankle pulsed with pain. But he knew only that he was hungry, and through his restless sleep he dreamed of feasts—of great banquets in which food was heaped and served in every imaginable way.

He awoke chilled and sick. There was no sun. A raw wind was blowing, and the first flurries of snow were whitening the hilltops. The air about him thickened and grew white while he made a fire and boiled more water. It was wet snow, half rain, and the flakes were large and soggy. At first they melted as soon as they came in contact with the earth, but more and more fell, covering the ground, putting out the fire, spoiling the supply of moss he used for fuel.

He strapped on his pack and stumbled forward, he knew not where. He was not concerned with the land of little sticks. He was not concerned with Bill, or with the hiding place by the river Dease. He was mastered by the verb "to eat." He was hunger-mad. He plunged ahead, now and then feeling down through the wet snow to grab at the watery muskeg berries, or to pull up some roots of grass. But it was all tasteless stuff that did not satisfy him. He found a weed that tasted sour and he ate all of it he could find, but it was not much, for it was hidden under several inches of snow.

He had no fire that night, nor hot water, and he crawled under the blanket to sleep the broken hunger-sleep. The snow turned into a cold rain. He awakened many times to feel it falling on his upturned face. Day came—a gray day and no sun. It had stopped raining. The sharp yearning of hunger was gone. There was a dull, heavy ache in his stomach, but it did not bother him so much. Once more he was mainly interested in the land of little sticks and the hiding place by the river Dease.

He ripped one of his blankets into strips and bound his bleeding feet. Also, he wrapped his injured ankle again. When it came time to prepare his pack, he paused for a long time over the small, heavy leather sack—but eventually it went along with him.

The snow had melted under the rain, and only the hilltops showed white. The sun came out and he looked around to get his bearings. He knew now that he was lost, but he sensed that he had wandered too far to the left, and so he set off to the right to correct his course.

Though the hunger pangs were no longer so intense, he realized that he was weak. He had to pause frequently for rest, and when he did so he attacked the muskeg berries and the patches of grass. His tongue felt dry and large, as though it was covered with hair, and it tasted bitter in his mouth. His heart gave him a great deal of trouble. When he had traveled a few minutes it would begin a remorseless thump, thump, thump, and then leap up and away in a painful flutter of beats that choked him and made him go faint and dizzy.

In the middle of the day he found two minnows in a large pool. It was impossible to bail it, but he was calmer now and managed to catch them in his tin bucket. In size, they were no longer than his little finger, but he was not particularly hungry. The dull ache

141

in his stomach had been growing duller and fainter. It seemed almost that his stomach was sleeping. He ate the fish raw, chewing them with painstaking care, for eating now was an act of pure reason. Actually, he had no desire to eat, but he knew that he must eat to live.

In the evening he caught three more minnows. He ate two and saved the third for breakfast. The sun had dried the moss, and he was able to build a fire and warm himself by drinking hot water. He had covered fewer than ten miles that day, and the next day, traveling whenever his heart permitted him, he covered less than five miles. But his stomach did not give him the slightest uneasiness. It had gone to sleep. He was in a strange country, too, and the caribou were growing more plentiful—also the wolves. Often their yelps drifted across the wilderness, and once he saw three of them slinking away near his path.

He made camp for the night, and in the morning, being more capable of reason, he untied the string that fastened the leather sack. From the sack he poured a yellow stream of coarse gold dust and nuggets. He divided the gold roughly in half, hiding one half in a piece of blanket, on a prominent ledge. The other half he returned to the sack. From his one remaining blanket, he ripped a few strips for his feet and ankle. He still clung to his gun, for there were bullets in that hiding place by the river Dease.

This was a day of fog, and this day hunger awoke in him again. He was very weak and it was common for him to stumble and fall. Once, as he moved across the swampy ground in the bottom of the valley, he slipped and fell squarely into a bird's nest. There were four tiny eggs, no more than a mouthful, and he ate them ravenously, crushing them between his teeth. But they only made his appetite sharper. He bobbed clumsily along on his injured ankle, making his way forward. As he did, looking down, he came upon footprints in the soggy moss. They were not his own—he could see that. They must be Bill's. Suddenly he was exhausted, utterly exhausted. He stumbled from weakness, and pitched forward on his face, cutting his cheek. Night was setting in. He did not move for a long time. Then he rolled over on his side, wound his watch, and lay there until morning.

He awoke to a day of heavy fog. Half of his last blanket he used as wrappings for his feet. Then he tried, but failed, to pick up Bill's trail. Really it did not matter, only—only—he wondered if Bill were lost, too. By midday his pack had begun to oppress him; it had become too heavy to bear. Again he divided the gold. This time he merely spilled half of it on the ground. In the afternoon he threw the rest of it away. He kept only the half blanket, the tin bucket, and the rifle.

Suddenly, a strange feeling, a kind of hallucination, or dream, began to trouble him. For some reason, he felt certain that he had one bullet. It was in the chamber of his rifle and he had overlooked it. On the other hand, he knew all the time that the rifle was empty. However, the thought that it was there persisted. He fought it off for hours, and then threw his rifle open and saw that it was empty. The disappointment was as bitter as though he had really expected to find the bullet.

He plodded on for half an hour. At times his mind wandered and he pushed on, like a machine, while strange thoughts gnawed at his brain. Again and again he was brought back to reality by the pangs of hunger. Once he saw a sight that nearly caused him to faint.

He reeled and swayed, and finally managed to keep himself from falling. Before him stood a horse. A horse! He could not believe his eyes. He rubbed his eyes savagely to clear the vision, and saw not a horse but a large brown bear. The animal was studying him with an unfriendly, a belligerent, curiosity.

The man had brought his gun halfway up to his shoulder before he realized that the rifle was empty. He lowered it and drew his hunting knife from its sheath at his hip. In front of him was meat and life! He ran his thumb along the edge of his knife. It was sharp. The point was sharp. He would fling himself upon the bear and kill it. But his heart began its warning thump, thump, thump, and he began to feel slightly dizzy.

His desperate courage was replaced by a surge of fear. He was weak, so weak—what if the animal attacked *him!* He drew himself up as tall as he could, gripping his knife and staring hard at the bear. The bear advanced slowly a couple of steps, reared up, and gave a low growl. If the man ran, he would run after him. But the man did not run. The man, too, growled savagely, terribly, giving voice to the fear that lay deep inside him.

The bear edged away to one side, growling menacingly as he did, himself confused by this mysterious creature that stood upright and unafraid. The man did not move. He stood like a statue until the bear finally slinked off, and then he began to tremble violently and sank down to the wet moss.

He pulled himself together and went on. He was afraid now in a new way. It was not the fear that he should die from lack of food, but that he should be destroyed fiercely before he even starved to death. There were wolves. Their howls drifted back and forth across the wilderness.

Now and then the wolves, in packs of two and three, crossed his path. But they stayed clear of him. They did not travel in large numbers, and besides, they were hunting the caribou which did not battle, while this strange creature that walked erect might scratch and bite.

In the late afternoon he came upon some scattered bones where the wolves had made a kill. An hour ago, this had been a caribou calf, frolicking and running about, very much alive. The man contemplated the bones, clean-picked and polished. Could it possibly be that he might end that way before the day was done? Such was life, eh? A vain and fleeting thing. It was only life that pained. There was no hurt in death. To die was to sleep. It meant peace, rest. Then why was he not content to die? Because he wanted to live! It was the life in him, unwilling to die, that drove him on.

But he did not think about this long. He crouched in the moss and placed a piece of caribou bone in his mouth. The taste was meaty and sweet. But his teeth lacked power, and so he crushed the bones between rocks, pounded them to a pulp, and then swallowed them.

He made his way onward. He crossed no more hills, but followed a large stream which flowed through a wide and shallow valley. He did not clearly see the stream or the valley. He saw nothing but visions, and moved as though in a dream. He rested whenever he fell, and once he lay panting on his side and closed his eyes.

He awoke lying on his back on a rocky ledge. The sun was shining bright and warm. He could think more clearly now. Off in the distance he heard the squawking of caribou calves. He had vague memories of rain and wind and snow, but whether he had been beaten by the storm for two days or two weeks he did not know.

For some time he lay on the ledge without moving, the sunshine pouring upon him, warming his beaten body. It was a fine day, he thought. With a painful effort he rolled over on his side. Below him flowed a wide and sluggish river. With his eyes he followed it slowly. He saw it rise toward the skyline and empty into a bright and shining sea. A *sea!*

Most unusual, he thought to himself— strange, a vision or a mirage—probably a vision, a trick of his troubled mind. He was certain of this when he saw a ship lying at anchor in the middle of the shining sea. He closed his eyes for a while, and then opened them. Strange how the vision persisted! He refused to permit himself to grow excited. He knew there were no seas or ships in the heart of this barren land—just as he had known there was no bullet in the empty rifle.

He heard a sound behind him, a half-choking gasp or cough. Very slowly he rolled over on his other side. He could see nothing, but he waited patiently. Again he heard a cough, and outlined between two jagged rocks, less than twenty feet away, he saw the gray head of a wolf. Its eyes were bleary and bloodshot and the head seemed to droop limply. The animal blinked in the sunlight. It seemed sick.

This, at least, he thought, was real. And he turned on his other side and looked in the direction of the vision. Amazing. The sea still shone in the distance and the ship could be clearly seen. Was it real after all? He closed his eyes for a long time while he thought. Then it came to him. He had been traveling *north,* away from the Dease and into the Coppermine Valley! This wide and sluggish river was the Coppermine. That

shining sea was the Arctic Ocean! The ship was a whaling ship lying in anchor in the gulf. It was all clear to him. It made sense!

He sat up and turned his attention to immediate affairs. His last blanket was gone and his feet were exposed and raw. Rifle and knife were both missing. He had lost his hat somewhere, with the bunch of matches in the band, but the matches against his chest were safe and dry. He looked at his watch. It showed eleven o'clock and was still running. Evidently he had kept it wound.

He was calm and collected. Though extremely weak, he had no sensation of pain. He was not hungry. The thought of food was not even pleasant to him, and whatever he did was fueled by the power of reason alone. He ripped off his pants legs to the knees and wrapped the material around his feet. Somehow he had managed to keep the tin bucket. He would have to have some hot water before he began what he knew would be a terrible journey to the ship.

His movements were slow, but he managed to collect some dry moss and to build a fire. After he had drunk a quart of hot water, he felt somewhat better. Even so, he could not walk for more than a minute or so without having to rest. That night, when the shining sea was blotted out by darkness, he knew that he was closer to it by perhaps four miles.

All throughout the night he heard the cough of the sick wolf, and he knew that the sick wolf clung to the sick man's trail in the hope that the man would die first. In the morning, on opening his eyes, he saw it watching him with longing, a wistful and hungry stare. It stood crouched with its tail between its legs, shivering in the chill of the morning. The wolf grinned weakly when the man spoke to it in a weak voice which was hardly louder than a hoarse whisper.

The sun rose brightly, and all morning the man stumbled toward the ship in the shining sea. The weather was perfect. It was the brief Indian summer of that region. It might last for a week. Tomorrow or the next day it might be gone.

In the afternoon the man came upon a trail. It was the trail of another man, one who did not walk, but who dragged himself on all fours. The man thought it might be Bill, but he was not particularly interested in this. He was interested in Life—the life that was in him which drove him on. He was very weary, but the life that was in him refused to die. It was because of this life that he still ate muskeg berries and minnows, and drank his hot water, and kept a wary eye on the sick wolf which stayed near.

He followed the trail of the other man until he came to the end of it—and saw a few fresh-picked bones near the footprints of many wolves. He saw a leather sack, exactly like his own, which had been torn apart by sharp teeth. He picked up the sack, though its weight was almost too much for his feeble fingers. Bill had carried it to the last. Ha! ha! He would have the laugh on Bill. He would survive and carry it to the ship on the shining sea. The man suddenly stopped and thought: How could he have the laugh on Bill if those bones were Bill's, if Bill was dead?

He turned away. Well, Bill had deserted him, but he would not take Bill's gold. And in disgust, he left the bones and staggered on.

That day he covered three miles and the next day two, for he was crawling now as Bill had crawled, and at the end of the fifth day the ship was still seven miles away, and he was unable to make even a mile a day. Still the good weather held, and he continued to crawl, though his knees, like his feet, had become raw. And all the time, the sick wolf coughed and wheezed at his heels.

Once, coming out of a faint, he heard a wheezing sound close to his ear. The wolf leaped lamely back, lost its footing, and fell. The man was not afraid. He was too far gone for that. But his mind was clear for the moment, and he lay on the ground and reasoned. The ship was no more then four miles away. He could see it quite clearly when he rubbed the haze out of his eyes. He could see, too, the white sail of a small boat in the water of the shining sea. But he could never crawl those four miles. He knew that. He knew that he could not crawl half a mile. And yet he wanted to live. It was unfair that he should die after all he had gone through. Fate asked too much of him. And though he was dying, he refused to die. It was madness, perhaps, but in the very grip of death, he defied death and refused to die.

Without moving, he lay on his back and gathered his strength. He could hear, slowly drawing nearer, the wheezing of the sick wolf's breath. It drew closer, ever closer, and he did not move. It was at his ear. His hands moved out—but they closed on empty air. The wolf backed away and waited.

For half a day the man lay motionless and waited, waited for the thing that wished to feed upon him and upon which he wished to feed. He did not hear the wolf's breath but as he came out of a dream he felt the tongue along his hand. He waited. The fangs pressed softly, the pressure increased as the wolf exerted its last strength in an effort to sink teeth in the food for which it had waited so long. But the man was ready, and his hand closed on the jaw. The other hand completed the grip. Slowly, while the wolf struggled feebly, he dragged the whole weight of his body on top of the wolf.

His hands were not strong enough to choke the wolf, but he was able to sink his teeth into the animal. He held on until he tasted a trickle of blood. He found strength in the force of his will and his love of life. At the end of half an hour, the wolf was dead. Later the man rolled over on his back and slept.

The men on the whaleship *Bedford* saw a strange object on the shore. It was moving slowly down the beach toward the water, squirming and writhing its way toward them at perhaps twenty feet an hour. The men climbed into the small boat and went ashore to see. They found something alive, but could hardly believe it was a man.

Three weeks later, the man rested in a bunk on the *Bedford*. With tears streaming down his cheeks, he told who he was and what he had undergone.

Soon after that he was able to sit at a table with the ship's officers. He gazed with awe and delight at the sight of so much food, but he grew nervous as it went into the mouths of others. As each mouthful disappeared, an expression of regret came into his eyes. He seemed quite sane except for one strange thing. He was haunted by the fear that there was not sufficient food aboard the boat. He repeatedly asked the cook and the captain about the supply of food. But no matter how many times they reassured him, he could not believe them.

The sailors noticed that the man was getting fat. He grew fatter every day. They limited his supply of food, but still he grew larger and fatter. Then one day, after breakfast, they watched him return to the table. He grabbed some rolls, looked at them the way a miser looks at gold, and thrust them under his shirt.

Later, in private, the sailors examined his bunk. Every nook and cranny was stuffed with food. The men shook their heads sadly and understood. They let him alone. He was simply preparing for another possible famine, that was all. The ship's doctor said he would recover from it—and he did, by the time the ship returned to San Francisco.

TELL ABOUT THE STORY. The following questions help you check your reading comprehension. Put an *x* in the box next to each correct answer.

1. The traveler in the wilderness was struggling against the handicap of
   ☐ a. a broken arm.
   ☐ b. an injured ankle.
   ☐ c. having no matches.

2. In order to stay alive, the man lived mainly on
   ☐ a. caribou meat.
   ☐ b. berries and boiled water.
   ☐ c. birds' eggs.

3. The man discouraged the bear from attacking him by
   ☐ a. firing the rifle at it.
   ☐ b. running away and hiding.
   ☐ c. growling savagely and refusing to move.

4. When the man first saw the sea and the ship, he thought that
   ☐ a. he must be dreaming or seeing things.
   ☐ b. it was a rescue ship that had been sent to save him.
   ☐ c. it was too far away to reach.

HANDLE NEW VOCABULARY WORDS. The following questions check your vocabulary skills. Put an *x* in the box next to each correct answer.

1. It was the last week of July or the first week of August—he did not know the precise date. The word *precise* means
   ☐ a. exact.
   ☐ b. final.
   ☐ c. first.

2. When the traveler finally found four tiny eggs, he ate them ravenously. Define the word *ravenously*.
   ☐ a. slowly or lazily
   ☐ b. greedily; very hungrily
   ☐ c. noisily; very loudly

3. The bear was studying the man with an unfriendly, belligerent curiosity. The word *belligerent* means
   ☐ a. helpful.
   ☐ b. young or youthful.
   ☐ c. interested in waging war.

4. The light of the sun was dimmed, almost obscured by the drifting mists and vapors. What is the meaning of the word *obscured*?
   ☐ a. increased
   ☐ b. fooled
   ☐ c. hidden

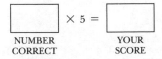

× 5 =

NUMBER
CORRECT

YOUR
SCORE

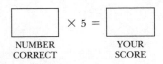

× 5 =

NUMBER
CORRECT

YOUR
SCORE

IDENTIFY STORY ELEMENTS. The following questions check your knowledge of story elements. Put an *x* in the box next to each correct answer.

1. Which phrase best describes the *setting* of the story?
   - ☐ a. noisy, crowded, and dirty
   - ☐ b. freezing, desolate, and wild
   - ☐ c. busy, sunny, and civilized

2. What happened first in the *plot* of the story?
   - ☐ a. The wolf attempted to kill the man.
   - ☐ b. The sailors noticed that the man was getting fat.
   - ☐ c. The man realized that Bill was gone.

3. Select the statement that best expresses the *theme* of the story.
   - ☐ a. A man's love of life provides him with the will to hold off death.
   - ☐ b. When you go on a long journey, you should make certain to bring enough food.
   - ☐ c. A man who deserts his partner in the wilderness deserves to die.

4. "Love of Life" best illustrates a *conflict*
   - ☐ a. with nature.
   - ☐ b. between two hated rivals.
   - ☐ c. that takes place in the mind of a character.

NOTE WORDS IN A PASSAGE. The following questions use the cloze technique to check your reading comprehension. Complete the paragraph by filling in each blank with one of the words listed below. Each word appears in the story. Since there are five words and four blanks, one of the words will not be used.

Many of Jack London's stories are set in the Yukon—a _____ in the northwestern part of Canada. During the Klondike Gold Rush of 1898, many prospectors rushed to this rugged and _____ territory in the hope of finding gold. Some were successful, but for most people the search resulted in _____ . They had to deal with severe hardships, including living in a climate that was often _____ cold.

desolate   disappointment

endured

bitterly   region

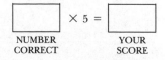

NUMBER CORRECT × 5 = YOUR SCORE

KNOW HOW TO READ CRITICALLY. The following questions check your critical thinking skills. Put an *x* in the box next to each correct answer.

1. Why did the traveler throw the gold away?
   - ☐ a. It was too heavy for him to carry.
   - ☐ b. He was already wealthy and didn't care about riches.
   - ☐ c. He thought nobody would believe it was really gold.

2. The traveler was probably able to kill the wolf because
   - ☐ a. he was still unusually strong.
   - ☐ b. the wolf was sick and not very strong.
   - ☐ c. he had a great deal of experience in fighting wolves.

3. When the sailors on the *Bedford* saw the figure on the shore, they could hardly believe it was a man. The situation suggests that
   - ☐ a. the sailors did not have good eyesight.
   - ☐ b. the traveler's appearance must have been horrible to behold.
   - ☐ c. the traveler looked reasonably well, considering the hardships he had endured.

4. At the end of the story, the man kept hiding food because he
   - ☐ a. was a thief.
   - ☐ b. planned to sell it when he arrived on shore.
   - ☐ c. was trying to guard against the terrible hunger he had recently known.

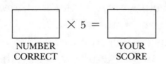

NUMBER   YOUR
CORRECT   SCORE

$\times 5 =$

Thinking for Writing and Discussion

- In "Love of Life," Jack London has created a powerful tribute to human determination and courage. Present evidence from the story to support that statement.
- When the traveler first saw the ship on the shining sea, he refused to become excited. Explain why the traveler felt that way.
- During the course of the story, the traveler confronted various animals, including birds, caribou, a bear, and a wolf. Describe one confrontation in which the man was successful, and one in which he was not.

Use the boxes below to total your scores for the exercises.

TELL ABOUT THE STORY

+

HANDLE NEW VOCABULARY WORDS

+

IDENTIFY STORY ELEMENTS

+

NOTE WORDS IN A PASSAGE

+

KNOW HOW TO READ CRITICALLY

▼

Total Score: Story 14

15. Spelling Bee

by Laurene Chambers Chinn

Meet the Author

Laurene Chambers Chinn (1902–1978) has written a number of very moving short stories, but she is best known for her novels. Although Chinn lived in Texas, she traveled widely in order to obtain the historical material that she used in her works. For example, while writing *Marcus,* a novel that deals with biblical themes, she journeyed to Greece, Israel, and Italy to do research. Chinn's other novels include *Believe My Love* and *Voice of the Lord.*

*W*ith the closing of the door, Ellen left one of her lives behind and entered upon the other. She moved slowly down the long flight of stairs that flanked the restaurant, and turned left toward the hotel.

"No use eating dinner there," Mama had protested. "You can eat at home and go later."

"We are supposed to have dinner at the hotel, Mama." Ellen spoke the word "Mama" in the Cantonese way, as if it were two words, with a quick, light stress on the second half. "When you are American, you do as Americans do."

"No harm being Chinese," Mama said.

Mama wasn't going to the high school with her tonight. Mama never went with her. On the street, Ellen shut out the world of home. This is easy when you speak Cantonese in one world and American in the other. Still, when you have won the county spelling bee, you can't help wanting your mother to watch you in the regional match. . . .

A big bus carried the thirty-five county champions from the dinner at the hotel to the high school. At eight o'clock the curtains parted revealing the audience to the boys and girls on stage. Thirty-five boys and girls on stage, thought Ellen, feeling a little bit sad, and thirty-four mothers in the audience. Henry was there, with his girlfriend, Dorothy. Now that Father was gone, Henry was head of the family. It ought to be enough that her brother was in the audience.

The teacher said, "*Botany,*" and smiled at Ellen. They had finished with the sixth-grade spelling books and were starting on the seventh. Twenty-eight girls and boys were still on stage.

"*Physician,*" said the teacher. Henry was a physician. Less than a year ago he had been an intern. He worked hard. It isn't easy to establish confidence when you wear an alien face.

"*Intense,*" Miss Kinsman said. If Mama had learned to speak English, maybe she wouldn't be so intensely shy. Mama had wrapped herself in her black sateen Chinese coat and trousers, wrapped herself also in her cloak of language, and refused to leave her kitchen even to buy groceries or a hat. Did Mama own a hat? Yes, Henry had bought one for her to wear at Father's funeral.

"*Tragedy,*" said Miss Kinsman. They were in eighth-grade spelling now, and nineteen contestants remained.

"*Tragedy,*" said Ellen, smiling at Miss Kinsman. "*T-r-a-g-e-d-y.*"

Mrs. Dillard had begun helping her after school when she became school champion, and they redoubled their labor after she won the county spelling bee. Mrs. Dillard had said, "Barring accidents, you might even win and represent our region at the national spelling bee in Washington."

Now, after an hour in the eighth-grade speller, with fewer than a dozen champions still on stage, Ellen was beginning to think Mrs. Dillard might be right. Ellen might win. Only a nitwit would want not to win. Well, then, she was a nitwit.

One of the judges rose. "Perhaps it is time to go into the old Blueback,"[1] he suggested.

A sigh rippled up among the contestants. Mrs. Dillard had taken Ellen all the way through the Blueback. "Trust your hunches," Mrs. Dillard had said, and her eyes had grown dreamy. "My goodness, I'd be proud to see a pupil of mine win the national spelling bee!"

But Ellen didn't want to go to Washington!

The teacher was smiling at Ellen. "*Deign.*"

The girl next to Ellen had just spelled *reign*. Ellen recalled the section, a group of words with silent *g*'s. Ellen spelled, "*D-a-n-e.*" She turned blindly to leave the stage. She had betrayed her talent for spelling, and she had betrayed Mrs. Dillard, and she had betrayed Henry.

"Just a minute," said Miss Kinsman. "I wanted you to spell *d-e-i-g-n*, meaning 'condescend,' but you have correctly spelled its homonym, and capital letters aren't necessary by the rules of the contest."

"O-o-o-h," wailed Ellen. It's a fine thing when you try to miss a word and can't. "Could I—could I have a drink, please?" she gulped.

The judge said, "We will have intermission until the bell rings."

With a whoop the champions scattered. Ellen hurried down the aisle toward Henry and Dorothy. Dorothy hugged her. "I had no idea you were so smart, little genius."

Henry said, "I'd be very proud to see you win, Ellen."

"I don't want to win." Suddenly she knew

---

1. **Blueback:** a spelling book.

151

why. She put the knowledge into a rush of words, speaking in Cantonese. "To go to Washington without my mother would advertise that she is old-fashioned and very shy and goes nowhere—not even here—with me."

Henry's face paled. His eyes turned from Ellen's and met Dorothy's. Ellen rushed into the hall. She wished the tears would quit coming in her eyes. She knew what she would do. She wouldn't win, but she would stay as long as she could without winning.

After three rounds in the Blueback, six contestants remained. Miss Kinsman turned to the "Words Difficult to Spell" section at the back. "*Abeyance*," she said.

Acerbity. Ache. Acquiesce. Amateur. Queer spellings remind you of other peoples in other times who have used these words in other ways. Language is a highway, linking all peoples and all ages. Mama was wrong to use language as a wall.

Caprice. Carouse. Catastrophe. . . .

Three contestants remained. Miss Kinsman turned to a page of words of seven and eight syllables. Henry was alone at the back now. Maybe Dorothy had got bored and gone home. Ellen thought of her mother. Thirty-four mothers had driven in from thirty-four neighboring counties, and Mama hadn't come six blocks to see the contest.

"*Incomprehensibility*," said Miss Kinsman. It was a lonely word. Things build up inside a person that other people don't comprehend. And people can't comprehend the shyness of a foreign-born mother unless they've had a foreign-born mother.

"*Indestructibility*," said Miss Kinsman. Ellen had risen, but she wasn't listening. Two people had come in at the back. One was Dorothy. The other was utterly familiar, yet, in the hat and dress, utterly strange. They went to sit beside Henry, and Mama was smiling at Ellen on the stage. Ellen had lived all her life with that loving smile.

"I'm sorry. I didn't hear the word." Turning to Miss Kinsman, Ellen raised her voice for the proud announcement, "My mother just came in."

"*Indestructibility*," said Miss Kinsman.

Ellen spelled the word clearly. Mama wouldn't understand, but this was a beginning. Mama had found the courage to come. Mama would find future courage—enough to become American. She had to win, now, and take Mama with her to the nation's capital. She and Mama would look at the buildings and the memorials. After such a trip, Mama would never hide away again.

If Mama could do what she had done tonight, Ellen could keep her wits about her for as long as it might take to be winner.

TELL ABOUT THE STORY. The following questions help you check your reading comprehension. Put an *x* in the box next to each correct answer.

1. At the beginning of the story, Ellen was upset because
   - ☐ a. she thought she hadn't studied enough for the spelling bee.
   - ☐ b. her mother didn't want her to enter the spelling bee.
   - ☐ c. her mother wasn't in the audience.

2. According to Ellen, her mother
   - ☐ a. was old-fashioned and shy.
   - ☐ b. was quite modern.
   - ☐ c. enjoyed making new friends.

3. When Ellen tried to miss a word on purpose, she
   - ☐ a. was criticized by Miss Kinsman.
   - ☐ b. was given another chance by the other students.
   - ☐ c. spelled its homonym correctly.

4. At the conclusion of the story, Ellen was determined to win the spelling bee in order to
   - ☐ a. make Mrs. Dillard proud.
   - ☐ b. take her mother to Washington.
   - ☐ c. gain fame and glory.

HANDLE NEW VOCABULARY WORDS. The following questions check your vocabulary skills. Put an *x* in the box next to each correct answer.

1. Before Henry became a physician, he worked as an intern. As used here, the word *intern* means
   - ☐ a. lawyer.
   - ☐ b. teacher.
   - ☐ c. doctor in training.

2. After three rounds in the spelling bee, six contestants remained. Define the word *contestants*.
   - ☐ a. people who judge a competition or contest
   - ☐ b. people who take part in a competition or contest
   - ☐ c. people who dislike a competition or contest

3. According to Ellen, people native to a country can't comprehend the shyness of a foreign-born person. What is the meaning of the word *comprehend*?
   - ☐ a. understand
   - ☐ b. oppose
   - ☐ c. remember

4. Only a nitwit wouldn't want to win the spelling bee. What is a *nitwit*?
   - ☐ a. a cheater
   - ☐ b. a scholar
   - ☐ c. a fool

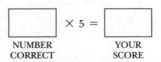

☐ × 5 = ☐

NUMBER CORRECT   YOUR SCORE

☐ × 5 = ☐

NUMBER CORRECT   YOUR SCORE

IDENTIFY STORY ELEMENTS. The following questions check your knowledge of story elements. Put an *x* in the box next to each correct answer.

1. The *main character* in "Spelling Bee" is
   - ☐ a. Ellen.
   - ☐ b. Mama.
   - ☐ c. Henry.

2. What happened last in the *plot* of the story?
   - ☐ a. Ellen decided to stay in the spelling bee for as long as she could without winning.
   - ☐ b. Mama smiled at Ellen on the stage.
   - ☐ c. Dorothy hugged Ellen and complimented her.

3. The *climax*, or turning point, of the story occurred when
   - ☐ a. Ellen asked for a drink of water.
   - ☐ b. Henry told Ellen he'd be proud to see her win.
   - ☐ c. Ellen saw her mother come in.

4. The *conflict* in "Spelling Bee" may best be described as
   - ☐ a. a clash with a force of nature.
   - ☐ b. an inner conflict that takes place in the mind of a character.
   - ☐ c. a conflict between two enemies who hate each other.

NOTE WORDS IN A PASSAGE. The following questions use the cloze technique to check your reading comprehension. Complete the paragraph by filling in each blank with one of the words listed below. Each word appears in the story. Since there are five words and four blanks, one of the words will not be used.

Words that people frequently have trouble spelling are usually called *spelling demons.* To master these "demons," spelling experts _____ looking carefully at the word, writing the word over and over, and dividing the word into _____ . You should also try to identify the _____ parts of the word and then focus on them. Sometimes you can find clues in the word to help you remember its correct _____ .

syllables   **champions**

spelling

suggest   **difficult**

☐	× 5 =	☐	
NUMBER CORRECT		YOUR SCORE	

☐	× 5 =	☐	
NUMBER CORRECT		YOUR SCORE	

KNOW HOW TO READ CRITICALLY. The following questions check your critical thinking skills. Put an *x* in the box next to each correct answer.

1. The last line of the story suggests that Ellen will
   ☐ a. win the spelling bee.
   ☐ b. finish second in the spelling bee.
   ☐ c. decide to drop out of the spelling bee.

2. Which statement is true?
   ☐ a. Seeing her mother in the audience made Ellen nervous.
   ☐ b. Seeing her mother in the audience made Ellen sad.
   ☐ c. Seeing her mother in the audience made Ellen want to win.

3. When she saw her mother come in, Ellen probably felt
   ☐ a. very confused.
   ☐ b. proud and pleased.
   ☐ c. disappointed.

4. We may infer that Ellen will
   ☐ a. encourage her mother to continue staying at home.
   ☐ b. change her mind about going to Washington with her mother.
   ☐ c. help her mother adjust and adapt to the United States.

Thinking for Writing and Discussion

- The opening paragraph of the story suggests that Ellen had two lives. Tell what they were and describe them briefly.
- Ellen thought, "Language is a highway linking all peoples and all ages. Mama was wrong to use language as a wall." How can language be a highway? A wall?
- Notice how the spelling words are used to introduce Ellen's thoughts. For example, when the teacher said *physician*, Ellen thought about her brother Henry, a physician. When the teacher said *intense*, Ellen thought about her mother's intense shyness. The last spelling word was *indestructibility*—unable to be destroyed. Why did the author conclude the story with that word?

Use the boxes below to total your scores for the exercises.

☐ **T**ELL ABOUT THE STORY
   +
☐ **H**ANDLE NEW VOCABULARY WORDS
   +
☐ **I**DENTIFY STORY ELEMENTS
   +
☐ **N**OTE WORDS IN A PASSAGE
   +
☐ **K**NOW HOW TO READ CRITICALLY
   ▼
☐ **Total Score:** Story 15

☐ × 5 = ☐

NUMBER   YOUR
CORRECT   SCORE

Acknowledgments

Acknowledgment is gratefully made to the following publishers, authors, and agents for permission to reprint these works. Adaptations and abridgments are by Burton Goodman.

"The Most Dangerous Game" by Richard Connell. © 1924 by Richard Connell. © renewed 1952 by Louise Fox Connell. Reprinted by permission of Brandt & Brandt Literary Agents, Inc.

"Raymond's Run" by Toni Cade Bambara. From *Gorilla, My Love* by Toni Cade Bambara. © 1970 by Toni Cade Bambara. Reprinted by permission of Random House, Inc.

"The Mother Goose Madman" by Betty Ren Wright. From July 1959 *Alfred Hitchcock's Mystery Magazine.* © renewed 1987 by Betty Ren Wright. Reprinted by permission of Larry Sternig Literary Agency.

"Split Cherry Tree" by Jesse Stuart. © 1938, renewed 1966 by Esquire, Inc. Reprinted by permission of the Jesse Stuart Foundation, P.O. Box 391, Ashland, Kentucky 41114.

"The Tiger's Heart" by Jim Kjelgaard. Reprinted by permission of Esquire, Inc.

"Martinez' Treasure" by Manuela Williams Crosno. Reprinted by permission of Manuela Williams Crosno.

"Ta-Na-E-Ka" by Mary Whitebird. Reprinted by permission of *Scholastic Voice.* © 1973 by Scholastic Magazines, Inc.

"All Summer in a Day" by Ray Bradbury. Reprinted by permission of Don Congdon Associates, Inc. © 1954, renewed 1982 by Ray Bradbury.

"Spelling Bee" by Laurene Chambers Chinn. All attempts have been made to locate the copyright holder.

Progress Chart

1. Write in your score for each exercise.
2. Write in your Total Score.

	T	H	I	N	K	TOTAL SCORE
Story 1						
Story 2						
Story 3						
Story 4						
Story 5						
Story 6						
Story 7						
Story 8						
Story 9						
Story 10						
Story 11						
Story 12						
Story 13						
Story 14						
Story 15						